Wh

Angus Robertson MP

with a foreword by Alex Salmond

First published in Great Britain in 2010 by
Biteback Publishing Ltd
Heal House
375 Kennington Lane
London
SE11 5QY

ISBN 978-1-84954-034-6

10 9 8 7 6 5 4 3 2 1

A CIP catalogue record for this book is available from the British Library.

Set in Garamond
Printed and bound in Great Britain by CPI Cox & Wyman, Reading, RG1 8EX.

Contents

Foreword

At this election Scotland can be the winner. Forget the phoney war between the London parties, what our nation needs is a strong team of Scottish MPs in the House of Commons – a team of SNP MPs who will stand up for their local area and protect the interests of the people of Scotland.

So why vote SNP? First and foremost, of all the parties, the SNP cares most about Scottish success. We are Scotland's Party and here at home, and in the parliament in London we offer Scotland the strongest voice.

SNP MPs will be effective local and national champions. We are of Scotland and for Scotland – in all its diversity – and work hard for the communities we represent.

When the SNP is successful, the London parties listen and that is crucial for our nation in the tough years ahead.

The London parties all offer the same thing – a dismal vision for our nation based on cuts and very different priorities. Tune into the election programmes, listen to the debates, and whether it is Tory, Labour or Liberal, they aren't talking about Scotland or the issues that matter most to people here. They aren't offering the solutions and ideas that can improve the quality of life for our families, neighbourhood and nation. For them Scotland is at best a second thought. They are more interested in their big battles than the needs of our communities. Our nation deserves better.

So at this election, with your help, we can make sure local communities get the best representation in London and that Scotland is heard. That is important on polling day, and even more important once the votes are counted and decisions are being taken at Westminster. Scotland's voice must not be missing, because if it is, people across Scotland – our neighbours and colleagues, our family and friends – will lose out.

As a party and as Scotland's government, our focus is first and foremost on winning the best deal for Scotland. We are working hard for economic recovery and new jobs and opportunities for our nation.

We are ambitious for you and your family and confident in Scotland's ability to succeed, now and with Independence. We know, with the right approach, and as long as we are not held back, our nation will once again prosper. And after the downturn, we are focused more than ever on building the stronger, more successful nation we know Scotland can be.

These elections are about giving you, your local area and Scotland the strongest possible voice in the decisions that will be taken in London.

Only SNP MPs will speak up for Scottish values. With your support we can step up efforts to support Scottish jobs. We can make a more powerful case to scrap the £5 billion ID card project and the £100 billion replacement for Trident so we can instead protect the vital local services we all rely on.

These are important elections. Too often it is the hard-working people and families who are left out and forgotten. This time, Scotland's voice can be heard.

Rt Hon. Alex Salmond MSP
Leader of the SNP and First Minister of Scotland
January 2010

Who we are

The SNP believes Scotland can be more successful. And we are working hard to make sure Scotland is not held back – that Scotland becomes the country we all know it can be.

Our approach is based on a vision of a better Scotland. We have total confidence in the people of this nation and know Scotland has the talent, ambition and opportunity to become one of the real success stories of this century. With your help and your support we can deliver on this vision.

As a party, we care about Scottish success. Government or election victory is not our end point or our purpose. Our winning post is a Scotland free to reach its full potential – a Scotland that is more prosperous, fairer, a voice for peace in the world – a Scotland that is independent. That principle – independence – is at our core. It means we work hard on jobs and the economy, on representing local communities, on dealing with crime and improving education and the health service, because if we earn your trust on these issues we can then earn your trust on independence. We are here to prove ourselves to you, and be a powerful voice on your behalf.

Our aim is to govern responsibly so we can continue to win your support. And through our Scottish MPs in the House of Commons and European MEPs in Brussels we will be a loud and effective voice for you, your community and our country. Our pledge is that we will always put the interests of people and communities here in Scotland first.

As the Scottish Government we are taking forward policies that embody Scotland's traditions of enterprise, democracy and social justice. We will always look for opportunities to enhance Scotland's position at home and in the wider world. At the heart of our approach is the delivery of higher levels of sustainable economic growth – creating a rich country and rich society – so that the Scotland that emerges from the downturn is wealthier, fairer and stronger. That is our purpose as a government and a party.

We offer a **social democratic contract** with the people of Scotland. It is a commitment built around core principles of solidarity, cohesion and sustainability:

- Solidarity – all of Scotland's citizens sharing in the opportunity and success
- Cohesion – no part of our country left behind
- Sustainability – passing on to the next generation a nation that is flourishing and living within its means.

Central to this approach is social partnership – that means we will work together across Scottish society. We know we don't have a monopoly of good ideas and will take forward the right ideas for Scotland, wherever they come from.

And we believe in greater responsibility for Scotland. Responsibility should rest with those best able to use it – in central or local government, or in our communities. Our approach will continue to bring about a culture of independence, a culture of responsibility, with the people of Scotland empowered whether at a national or local level. We want to ensure communities and individuals are playing their part in efforts to deal with some of the most pressing challenges facing our nation, from the current economic downturn to the longer-term problems associated with alcohol misuse.

And of course just as greater responsibility for communities and individuals can bring benefits to society as a whole, so too can greater responsibility and independence for our nation.

Later in this book we explore in more detail what these principles mean to us and how they influence our actions as a party. And we will take you through the various beliefs, policies and initiatives that offer the reason why you should vote SNP.

Alex Salmond sets out the SNP's approach to government, May 2007

This parliament, created by the people of Scotland in a referendum, is bigger than any of its members or any one party. I believe that Scotland is ready for change and for reform. This is a small nation with a big future. But it is also a small nation with big challenges.

Certainly, the gap between rich and poor is too great. We need to grow faster. We need to heal the scars of the past. We need to be greener. We need to be still smarter.

We have a sense of ourselves. A sense of community and, above all, a sense of the 'common weal' of Scotland.

Of course, in this part of the chamber we seek independence and equality for Scotland – not everyone agrees. But there is a broad consensus on the need for this parliament to assume greater responsibility for the governance of Scotland. There is an understanding that we are engaged in a process of self-government – and an awareness of the distance we have already travelled.

The nature and composition of this third Scottish Parliament makes it imperative that this government will rely on the strength of its argument in parliament and not the argument of parliamentary strength. Despite all the challenges we will face together, I welcome that as a chance to develop a new and fundamentally more reflective model of democracy.

> Let me say to Parliament that what matters to the people we all represent is less the structure of government and more what we, all of us, achieve on the people's behalf.
>
> In this century, there are limits to what governments can achieve. But one thing any government I lead will never lack is ambition for Scotland. Today I commit myself to leadership wholly and exclusively in the Scottish national interest. We will appeal for support policy by policy across this chamber. That is the parliament the people of Scotland have elected, and that is the government that I will be proud to lead.

What we believe in

In a speech in October 2009, Alex Salmond MP set out some of the essential elements of the SNP:

Just over two years ago we became the government of Scotland. That happened because we offered our vision of a more successful country. We said to the people of our nation that there should be no limits on Scotland's achievement, on Scottish success.

Since 2007 the world has tilted on its financial axis but we can win again by offering the same contract to the people in communities across our nation. A contract based on our social democratic values – wealth created and wealth shared. The creation of wealth is important when times are good. It is imperative when times are tough. The sharing of wealth is important when times are good. It is a moral imperative when times are tough.

Our contract was based on the sure and certain knowledge that we, the SNP, will always put the people of this nation first – creating a rich country and rich society. Each and every SNP MP elected next year, will join each and every SNP councillor, MSP and minister, member and supporter in this great project to make our nation the place we all know it can be. To improve the quality of life and life chances of Scots young and old; to protect and support the people of our nation, strong and weak, and to be Scotland's voice, Scotland's party, north, south, east and west, in Holyrood and Westminster.

This is who we are and what we believe in. As a party we have been working for Scotland and local communities for over seventy years. We are proud to have been a powerful voice for the people of this country in good times and bad, the party that cares most about Scottish success and winning the best deal for our citizens and our communities. We are of Scotland and for Scotland.

At our core the SNP believes in Scotland's potential. We have clear ambitions for our nation. We have no doubt Scotland can be a better place now and in the future. That means we are working hard to improve the quality of life for families and communities across Scotland, and we are determined to do more, both with the current responsibilities of the Scottish Parliament and when Scotland becomes independent.

Our nation can be healthier. The SNP has kept vital health services local. We are now investing in new community health facilities across Scotland so that healthcare is modern, fast and close to home. With independence we will be able to act more effectively to tackle drug and alcohol abuse and tackle the poverty that blights too many communities and is the root cause of so much ill health.

Families in Scotland can be wealthier. An SNP government has removed the burden of business rates from thousands of small businesses, freeing them to grow and create more and better paid jobs. We are now investing £220 million more to give Scottish businesses a competitive advantage so they can create new and better jobs. With independence, we will be able to lower corporation tax so that Scotland can become an even more attractive location for growing businesses.

Local communities can be safer. The SNP government has put more police on our streets to detect and deter crime. We are taking forward plans to clamp down on the cheap booze that fuels so much of the anti-social behaviour and crime in our communities. And with more responsibilities for the Scottish Parliament we will finally be able to act against air weapons, by controlling their use.

Our nation can be fairer. We have introduced free, healthy school meals for thousands more pupils from low-income families. And we are providing the money to freeze the council tax again next year – welcome relief after the doubling of local tax under Labour and Tory governments. This will leave more money in people's pockets as we emerge from recession and protect groups such as Scottish pensioners who live on fixed incomes.

Life should be easier for young families. The SNP has already increased the amount of free nursery education available for three- and four-year-olds with plans to increase this further next year. And with independence we will be able to do more, with our ambition to match the universal childcare support available in similar nations in Scandinavia.

Scotland can be greener. The SNP government has made clear our opposition to the building of new nuclear power stations in Scotland. We have passed the world's most ambitious climate change legislation and are turning this world-leading law into effective action. And with a stronger parliament we can do more to invest in Scotland's renewable and carbon capture potential so that our nation becomes a European and world leader in these technologies, creating thousands of new green jobs.

Scotland can be smarter. We are building more schools at a faster rate than previous administrations and class sizes are at a record low. In the year ahead we are introducing new support for students to increase their income. With greater responsibilities for our parliament, we can act to more effectively integrate skills training and employment so that Scotland can develop an increasingly skilled workforce.

Putting principles into action

It is important that people understand who we are and what we believe in because those principles underpin our decisions as campaigners in your community, as the Scottish Government, as councillors in local authorities across Scotland and as Scottish MPs, MSPs and MEPs at Westminster and Holyrood and in Europe. They have guided us in the decisions we have taken to date and the decisions we will have to take as we deal with the impact of the recession on our country and public finances. And they will guide us as we manage the significant cuts in public spending now planned by the government in London.

These principles will determine how we vote on issues of importance in the Scottish Parliament, the House of Commons and the European Parliament to protect and promote Scottish interests. They also provide a clear indication of the sort of country we would

like to build with new responsibilities for the Scottish Parliament
and with independence.

Our social democratic contract

We continue to focus on growing Scotland's economy because that
will bring greater prosperity to families and communities throughout
Scotland and allow us to invest more to create the rich society that
Scotland can be. That is our social democratic contract with the
people of this nation.

Having higher aspirations for Scotland is about being ambitious
for the wellbeing of our people. At the moment the system leaves
some people as winners – those at the top and those who know how
to play the system. We want ordinary Scots and their families to get
their fair share.

Our social democratic contract is based on creating the wealth
to deliver excellent public services and good social provision. Since
the SNP took office this has been illustrated by our decisions to
keep and enhance children's cancer services in Edinburgh, Glasgow,
Aberdeen and Dundee, our determination to put 1,000 more police
officers on the streets to make communities safer, our extension
of free nursery hours for thousands of pre-school children and
giving the go-ahead for the new hospital on the site of the current
Southern General Hospital in Glasgow.

Scotland has a long and proud tradition of supporting fairness,
justice and compassion. We have upheld and built on these
important elements of our society by cutting prescription charges –
a tax on ill health – as a first step on the road to getting rid of them
by 2011, extending provision of free, nutritious school meals for
children from poorer backgrounds, protecting and expanding the
concessionary bus scheme and freezing the council tax, easing the
financial pressure on families and individuals at this difficult time.

And we are determined to see all parts of the country share in our nation's wealth. That's why we introduced the road equivalent tariff for ferry journeys to the Western Isles, reducing the barriers to growth put in place by high transport costs. The benefits of this policy are being seen, with thousands more tourists now visiting the isles. It is why we are investing to reduce journey times by rail between Inverness, Aberdeen and the Central Belt and to support the rural economy through our £1.6 billion Rural Development Programme. And it is why SNP MPs in the House of Commons will continue to work hard to protect community post offices both in rural and urban Scotland and to maintain the Royal Mail's universal delivery obligation.

And as we look ahead to a period of significant reductions in public spending, our social democratic contract means we will argue in the House of Commons for certain priorities. We will be a powerful voice for the issues that matter most to communities and individuals across our nation.

Instead of wasting billions on a new nuclear missile system, the next parliament must, for example, protect the incomes of Scottish pensioners. We need Scottish MPs arguing to cut Trident and abandon plans to spend £5 billion on 'Big Brother' ID cards and making the case for fair and proper increases to the state pension so that it rises each year in line with earnings.

There are important choices to be made and in Scotland our Budget for this year is protecting frontline services. And as we emerge from recession it is putting in place new support for Scottish businesses so they can grow and employ more people. Cuts have had to be made and our choice was to halt spending on the Glasgow airport rail link and government bureaucracy so we could continue to deliver better local healthcare and replace more poor-condition schools.

These choices are not easy. They are designed to deliver the biggest benefit now and in the medium term for more people across Scotland. And despite calls from some to scrap free care for the elderly in order to fund the airport rail link, we knew our contract with the people would not allow us to cut this crucial care for thousands of the most vulnerable Scots.

Social partnership

We also know that as a party and government we do not have a monopoly on good ideas and that if Scotland is to reach its full potential, we must engage with all parts of society and all political views to deliver the most effective policy choices.

And so we have worked with organisations such as the Scottish TUC and the Federation of Small Business to deliver policies designed to improve our nation's skills and remove some of the heavy financial burdens facing the businesses that form the lifeblood of so many local communities. We have listened to the views of the Green Party to take forward a scheme to provide insulation in tens of thousands of Scottish homes – helping families reduce their energy bills and enabling Scotland to cut its carbon emissions.

Our decision to reduce prescription charges followed the advice of the many charities that support Scots living with long-term conditions, and our plans to deliver new financial support for hard-pressed students followed detailed consultation and discussion with the National Union of Students and others. We know this is the right approach and will help ensure that the decisions we do take in the years ahead reflect a broader consensus across our nation.

And of course through the National Conversation we have been engaged in the biggest consultation of its type on the future direction of our country and we believe the people of Scotland should have their say on whether or not our parliament gains new responsibilities.

Culture of independence

Independence is part of who we are, but independence is not an end in itself; it is one part of our desire to create a more successful Scotland. Independence also reflects our belief that as a nation, as a community or as individuals, we will do best when we take responsibility for our own success. That is at the heart of our efforts to build a new culture of independence and responsibility in Scotland. We want to empower communities and individuals, alongside empowering our nation, so that Scotland reaches its full potential.

In a speech to the SNP 2006 spring conference, Nicola Sturgeon MSP said: 'We will offer a new, a better, a more exciting and a more engaging vision of the future – a vision of independence: independence for Scotland and for everyone who lives in Scotland; a vision of ambition and achievement; a Scotland where anything and everything is possible if we try hard enough.'

As a party we are looking to respond to the new confidence and ambition of the people of Scotland, and trying to capture that spirit in the work of the Scottish Government. Even though we have faced a deep recession and real challenges, there is a clear sense in Scotland that together we can emerge stronger. Together we can learn the lessons from this recession and build a country better suited to our needs and better able to seize the opportunities that will emerge as we recover and our economy grows.

We believe wholeheartedly in greater responsibility for Scotland. Responsibility should lie with those best able to use it – in central or local government, or in our communities. We want to bring about this culture of independence, this culture of responsibility, to ensure communities and individuals can play their part in building a rich country and rich society, turning our purpose – higher levels of sustainable economic growth – into a reality. And it presents a challenge to all of us – parliament, communities, individuals – to play our part in tackling some of the deep rooted problems in our society including poverty and the misuse of alcohol.

This principle sits at the heart of our actions as a party and government. In our health service, we are looking to give communities a bigger say in their local health service through elections to Scotland's health boards. In the battle against climate change we have set up a community Climate Challenge Fund to support the work that goes on at a local level to reduce our carbon emissions. And in government, our concordat with local government has delivered a new, more effective partnership between central and local government that is helping us deliver, together, new strategies on poverty, early years and healthy living.

The SNP trusts the people of Scotland. The more we can do close to home, the better our country will be.

Community campaigners

Effective local campaigning is central to our approach as a party across Scotland. We are determined to stand up for Scotland and the people and communities we represent.

And in this election to the House of Commons, it is more important than ever that the people of Scotland have effective representation. The SNP gives Scotland and our communities a stronger voice in Westminster. Without the SNP, Scottish concerns would be forgotten. And the more MPs we have the more we can achieve. With your vote and your support, a bloc of twenty Scottish MPs from the Scottish National Party can win important concessions and victories for Scotland in the next parliament.

Six SNP MPs were returned after the 2005 election, with John Mason joining the team after his stunning by-election victory in Glasgow East in 2008. Over the life of this parliament, the SNP group have worked hard for their constituents and communities and put Scotland's priorities first.

Angus MP Mike Weir has championed consumer concerns – demanding an investigation into the workings of the energy market, seeking improved regulation and compensation for the victims of Farepak, and heaping pressure on the Labour government over proposals to privatise the Royal Mail. He has been at the forefront of local and national campaigns to save local post offices and Post Office services.

Mike's battle with the energy regulator, Ofgem, over the discriminatory transmission charges faced by Scottish energy generators continues and, along with Alex Salmond, he has been fighting for Scotland to secure access to the near £200 million that is lying untouched – and at present unusable – in the fossil fuel levy fund. That is money that should be delivering green jobs throughout Scotland.

Mike has also been in the vanguard of Scottish MPs campaigning against the folly of the Westminster Government's proposals to create a tax hike for owners of self-catering cottages, a major source of employment in many areas of rural Scotland.

Pete Wishart, MP for Perth & North Perthshire, serves on the Scottish Affairs Select Committee in the House of Commons, where he has interrogated bank bosses about financial sector bonuses. He has also exposed the madness of the UK government's plans to spend £5 billion on 'Big Brother' ID cards when cuts are being proposed in Scotland's budget.

In sport, Pete has led the charge at Westminster against Gordon Brown's plans for a British football team – plans that threaten the future of the Scottish football team. He is also arguing for the 2014

Glasgow Commonwealth Games to enjoy the same advantages and support as the London Olympics – specific support from the National Lottery and more money to spend on regeneration projects in and around the Commonwealth Games sites. Again, this would bring a jobs boost in those communities and wider economic benefit across Scotland from an event that will be a wonderful showcase for our nation.

Soaring fuel prices is an issue of continuing concern for many businesses and individuals across Scotland, and Na h-Eileanan an Iar MP Angus MacNeil has been working with bodies such as the Road Hauliers Association to press for the introduction of a fuel duty regulator. This would see the revenue raised from VAT on higher fuel prices recycled to reduce the duty we pay on petrol and diesel. The result would be a mechanism that protects hard-pressed motorists and businesses from soaring forecourt prices.

Angus has also worked with local campaigners and the local MSP, Alasdair Allan, to persuade the MoD to reverse their plans to shed 125 defence jobs at the Uist rocket range – jobs that are vital to the fragile local economy.

John Mason, MP for Glasgow East, was elected in a by-election just over half way through the current parliament. In that by-election he promised to be a 'local and vocal' MP and he has been working hard to deliver – using every opportunity to stand up for his constituents in Glasgow. He has been pressing the London government to do more to get people back into employment and arguing that benefit reforms must be about sorting the system, not demonising and punishing people left unemployed by the recession.

Most recently he has highlighted the threat to attendance allowance resulting from the UK government's plans to extend care for the elderly in England. The English system will not match the free care in Scotland, but to pay for the reform, support could be removed from thousands of disabled Scots. Figures from the Department for Work and Pensions and the Institute for Social and Economic Research (ISER) show that 167,940 people in Scotland receive attendance allowance. Independent research by ISER shows that removing the allowance would push 40 per cent of those people – 67,000 Scots – into poverty.

Stewart Hosie, MP for Dundee East, speaks for the SNP on finance and the economy. Given the perilous state of the public finances, he has been pressing the Treasury on the growing UK budget deficit. Working with Scotland's Finance Secretary, John Swinney, on the wider budgetary issues, Stewart has been challenging the UK government on its plans to slash spending this year – a move that will endanger thousands of jobs and weaken recovery. In a speech in the House of Commons on 20 April 2009, he said:

> Slashing public spending in the teeth of recession will only add to the anxiety of households and high streets. This dangerous move will seriously set back economic recovery.
>
> The Chancellor must look to America, where President Obama has introduced an economic stimulus package worth $787 billion and more than half of that is being spent at state level. The state of Maryland, for example – which has a similar population to Scotland – will receive some £2.6 billion extra funding, supporting 66,000 jobs over the next two years. Yet in the UK, Alistair Darling's Budget is proposing to cut Scottish public spending from 2010 by £500 million a year, which would destroy 8,700 jobs in Scotland.
>
> There is clear blue water the width of the Atlantic between President Obama's stimulus package, which will support some 3.5 million jobs nationwide, and the budget-cutting response of Labour.

Stewart has also been one of the most vocal MPs in support of the campaigns for fairer taxation for Scotch whisky and for bingo clubs – ending the discriminatory taxation that sees Scotch taxed at a higher rate than other alcohol and bingo facing almost 50 per cent higher taxation than other forms of gambling.

After twenty-three years representing the people of Banff & Buchan, Alex Salmond, SNP leader and First Minister, is standing down as an MP this year. In London, Alex has been a powerful advocate for Scotland and the communities he represents. Over the years he has ensured that the interests of Scotland's fishing industry could not be forgotten in the House of Commons and he now leads the first Scottish government that has given this economically important sector the priority it deserves.

Alex was also one of the strongest voices in the House of Commons against the illegal invasion of Iraq and led efforts to hold Tony Blair to account for taking the UK to war on a false prospectus. Over the years he has stood up for Scottish interests at every opportunity, arguing forcefully on issues as diverse as opposition to the poll tax, increased investment in jobs and economic recovery, and incentives to maximise production from North Sea oil and gas.

I have been an MP for nine years now and in that time have come to appreciate the vital importance of an MP's role as champion of local causes. Working to help constituents and standing alongside local campaigners are two of the most rewarding aspects of an MP's job.

As MP for Moray, home to two RAF bases, I have been determined to champion veterans' welfare issues, and behind the scenes have brokered reforms that will allow inquiries into the accidental deaths abroad of military personnel to be held in Scotland for the first time. And as the SNP's defence spokesperson, I will continue to work for the men and women, from my constituency and from across our country, who are currently serving with such dedication in Afghanistan, to make sure they have the equipment they need to keep them safe.

These are just some examples of campaigns that have been taken forward with passion and determination – and some success – by SNP MPs in the House of Commons as part of the wider SNP team. We have worked with constituents, councillors and MSPs to give a strong voice to national, local and in some cases very personal campaigns.

This is at the heart of our job as members of Parliament. We know we are elected to stand up for Scotland and just as importantly to fight and win for the people we represent.

Scotland's journey

Scotland is on a journey to greater self-determination and independence and it is the people of Scotland who will decide how far and how quickly our nation travels along that road.

Already, with the restoration of the Scottish Parliament in 1999, Scotland has taken responsibility for many of its domestic affairs and the debate is no longer focused on whether or not the Scottish Parliament should exist. Now it is about how many new responsibilities our parliament should have and whether Scotland becomes, once again, an independent nation.

The Union of the Crowns in 1603 and the Treaty of Union of 1707 created the United Kingdom, bringing together the previously independent nations of Scotland and England into a single state. And over the last 150 years the Scots have been looking to redefine their role within the UK and the nature of their relationship with the other nations of these isles.

It is a journey rooted in a central principle of Scottish constitutional law – that the people are sovereign. As the Claim of Right of 1988 made clear, it is 'the sovereign right of the Scottish people to determine the form of government best suited to their needs', echoing the words of the Declaration of Arbroath almost seven centuries earlier.

The first step on that journey was the creation of the Scottish Office and the position of Secretary of State for Scotland, to represent Scottish interests. The Scottish Office gained administrative responsibility for a range of domestic affairs while legislative responsibility remained in Westminster. Calls for a Scottish parliament or assembly grew from the end of the nineteenth century, with a Scottish Home Rule Bill passing its initial parliamentary stage in 1913.

The creation of the Scottish National Party (SNP) in 1934 and the work of the Scottish Covenant Association (SCA) made sure the issue of home rule and independence remained part of the political debate in Scotland; indeed, the SCA secured two million signatures in favour of a Scottish parliament between 1949 and 1950. However, it was Winnie Ewing's victory for the SNP in the 1967 Hamilton by-election that put the issue of Scotland's place in the UK at the top of the political agenda.

The Hamilton by-election forced the London parties to come forward with their own schemes for Scottish devolution and led directly to the referendum of 1979. A majority of Scots voted in

Alex Salmond on the Declaration of Arbroath, April 2008

Today, within the present constitutional settlement, we do our utmost to improve the lives of the people of Scotland. And we know that, tomorrow, with full responsibility for our destiny, we can make Scotland an even better nation, our people freer, more prosperous and more secure.

That is our vision. And it is the same vision that Thomas Jefferson showed America in the Declaration of Independence, a declaration that was steeped in the principles of the Enlightenment – an intellectual revolution that Scots did so much to shape.

Some scholars also argue that Jefferson and the other founders of the republic themselves drew on a much earlier inspiration – the Declaration of Arbroath, which encapsulated the resolve of Scotland's 'community of the realm' in 1320. That after all was the inspiration ten years ago for Tartan Day, and Scotland Week was a Senate resolution asserting that the Declaration of Independence was 'modelled' on the Arbroath Declaration. However, Arbroath was not only a ringing declaration of the fundamental rights and integrity of an independent Scotland, but arguably Europe's first statement of a contractual relationship between government and governed.

When the community of the realm articulated the view that they would back the monarch to defend their rights, but would remove him if he failed to do so, they embarked on a road which led to America four and a half centuries later where the Arbroath Declaration was echoed with equal clarity and force. And it is that echo which we hear today in Scotland – in the twenty-first century, as we consider our nation's future.

It is to America that we can look to see the power of independence and the importance of democratic principles. It is to Thomas Jefferson that we can we look for guidance on the principles and conduct of our national debate.

And it is the words of Thomas Jefferson that will inspire us – today and in the years ahead: 'We are a people capable of self-government, and worthy of it.'

favour of a Scottish assembly at that time. However, the proposal fell as a result of the 40 per cent rule, which required not only a majority 'yes' vote but also 40 per cent of all those on the electoral register to vote in favour.

It was not until 1997, when Scots were given the opportunity to vote again on devolution, that the Scottish Parliament we know today was approved by an overwhelming three-quarters of the Scottish electorate. It was established in 1999 with responsibility for a wide range of Scottish domestic affairs. And over the past decade it has taken on new responsibilities including freedom of information and many aspects of our railways.

Now, every party in the parliament and the majority of Scots surveyed believe that the parliament should extend its responsibilities further. People recognise the areas where Scotland is held back by decisions taken in London and there is a belief that we could achieve so much more if we were able to take these decisions ourselves.

Some believe that the parliament should only take on a small number of new responsibilities, including those set out by the recent Calman Commission on Scottish Devolution covering air weapons, drink-driving and speed limits. The SNP supports the transfer of these additional responsibilities and in government has published the legislation that could make this happen quickly.

Others believe the parliament can best serve Scotland by taking on substantial new responsibilities including our economy and public finances. This would enable Scotland to respond more effectively to economic pressures and speed our nation's recovery. And, of course, with independence, Scotland would be able to do even more. These options were explored in the SNP government's National Conversation.

We are now more than ten years into devolution. It is time to reflect on Scotland's journey to this point and the path we should follow to secure the best future, the most successful future for our nation. In a speech to celebrate the tenth anniversary of the Scottish Parliament, Alex Salmond said:

The decade since this parliament was reconvened has proven to be a remarkable time in our political history, a time in which there have been some notable legislative successes. Scotland led the UK in banning smoking in public places, and will lead the world in reducing carbon emissions. These are things in which all Scots should take great pride.

But success should also be judged by the way the parliament has gone about its business, how it has woven itself into the tartan of Scottish society, how we have carried ourselves, how we have become a parliament worthy of the name and worthy of the nation.

The Scottish Parliament is founded on transparency, and inclusivity for all the people of Scotland. Proportional representation has made the parliament genuinely representative of the range of views in Scotland. That electoral system has resulted in two coalition governments followed by a minority government. We have certainly broken the mould – learning how to build a system of governance that reflects and responds to the values of our people.

Some said it could not be done, that the parliament was bound to fail, born to fail. But we have – as a parliament and as a people – proven them to be wrong.

This parliament has found its place in Scottish society. It is no longer 'new' in the eyes of our people. In fact, it has become so familiar that many now struggle to recall what it was like not to have a Scottish Parliament.

Today we are right to celebrate the successes of the parliament thus far. We also, rightly, consider its future. The Scottish Parliament is here to stay – this much we know, but the reconvening of this parliament was never an event but a process.

Following its first decade, this country is reflecting on how, together, we can meet the challenges of the next decade and of those to come. There are different visions, different proposals. But at the heart of each is a genuine regard for what is best for the future of Scotland. In searching for the solutions we believe are best for Scotland, we share a common purpose. And that exchange of ideas, taking place here in Scotland, is the sign of a healthy, thriving democracy.

Scotland's potential

When the Treaty of Union was signed in 1707, fifteen of the twenty-five articles related to the economy. Three hundred years later, as we assess the next steps for Scotland, the economy is once again at the heart of the reform that we need.

According to the International Monetary Fund, the United Kingdom has one of the most centralised economies in the developed world. Scotland has responsibility for less than 15 per cent of its finances; London controls the rest. That means decisions taken in London can and do hold Scotland back. They can and do prevent us from reaching our full potential.

There was a time when Australia, Canada, Ireland and the United States were all run from London. They are all now wealthier per person than the economically centralised UK. And none of these nations would choose to let London decide what was best for them today.

The London government operates a one-size-fits-all approach that is ill suited to our needs. This has led to lower than average economic growth in Scotland for generations, despite all our relative advantages in terms of skills and resources.

When we write about economic growth, what we are really writing about is jobs and opportunities: what jobs are open to our people and what opportunities exist in our communities. The global downturn has made clear that employment statistics are not just statistics – they tell a story of what is happening in homes across the country. Behind each number is a real life and a unique experience. That's why we need to get our economic policy right, now and for the future.

The global downturn has also made clear that the countries that emerge the strongest will be the ones that innovate and find solutions matched to their strengths and the ingenuity of their people. In Scotland, we should be optimistic about our future. Scotland is a land of inventors and entrepreneurs. We have had low economic growth over the last generation, but that has not always been the case. And what we know for certain is that while we might be currently living in a low-growth economy, the Scots are not a low-growth people. The country of Fleming and Watt is the same country that is pushing the boundaries with research in new life-saving medicines and planet-saving energy solutions.

One of the brightest opportunities for Scotland's economic future can be found in energy. In the 1970s, commercial oil extraction began in the North Sea. Since then, we have sent £269 billion to the Exchequer in London. More oil has been extracted from Scottish waters than from Norwegian waters. And while we can take great pride in our industry, we have not been nearly so well served by our political leadership. While Norway was saving, the UK Treasury was spending. The Norwegian Oil Fund now sits at a massive £274 billion – the equivalent of £57,000 per person.

With 25 billion barrels of oil remaining – with a wholesale value estimated at up to £1 trillion – it is critical that we start making the most of what is left. That means acting responsibly now so the benefit of the remaining oil wealth can be enjoyed by Scots today and the benefits extended for future generations. Like Norway, Scotland needs an oil fund. Norway's first payment into its oil fund was only £195 million, back in 1996. The lesson here is that we can start small, but we must start. We look in more detail at oil funds in Norway and elsewhere later in this book.

Of course, Scotland has been blessed twice. Our energy future lies in more than hydrocarbons – it rests also in the vast potential of renewable energy around our shores. Scotland has 25 per cent of Europe's wind potential, 25 per cent of its tidal potential and 10 per cent of its wave potential. And we must act now to secure Scotland's renewable energy future.

With the same tax and regulatory responsibilities as other, independent countries, not only can we prolong the life of hydrocarbons, we can also set up incentives for development and knowledge transfer into renewables. We can end discriminatory transmission charging, make the critical decisions on carbon capture, work towards a European supergrid and begin to save in an oil and energy fund. Today, we are limited in what we can do to take forward each of these ambitions. Scotland is being held back at the expense of jobs and increased wealth across our nation. A Scottish Government with the appropriate levers could do so much more to invest in our energy potential offshore.

The same applies to the actions we could and should take to bring businesses to our cities and town centres. Already within our current responsibilities, the SNP in government is making a difference to Scottish businesses. We have cut business rates for tens of thousands of small businesses across Scotland – ensuring that many of our country's smallest pay no rates at all. And we are delivering a £220 million competitive advantage by ensuring Scottish business rates bills are lower than those elsewhere in the UK.

But there is so much more we could do to support businesses as they look to grow and create new and better-paid jobs. If we had the same tools at our disposal as our neighbouring countries, Scotland's economy would be more successful.

Scotland as part of the UK has a corporation tax rate that leaves us at a distinct competitive disadvantage, as the graph below shows.

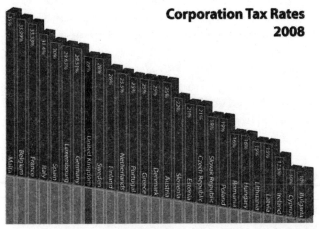

Corporation Tax Rates 2008

Source: KPMG's Corporate and Indirect Tax Rate Survey, 2008

Ireland, Finland and Austria are just a few examples of comparably sized countries that have given themselves a huge advantage by cutting their corporation tax rates. And while these countries have cut their tax rates, they have actually increased their total tax revenue, by drawing in new companies, new headquarters and high-value jobs.

There is a knock-on benefit to this, too, as headquarters bring research and development, which in turn leads to a new wave of entrepreneurs who leave the big companies to start new ones.

This kind of policy on business taxes and employment growth shows what happens when SNP politicians are in a position to deliver for Scotland. In government we can do something tangible for tens of thousands of businesses via the Small Business Bonus

Scheme, and with more responsibilities over the economy there is so much more we could achieve with a competitive corporation tax rate.

By sending more MPs to Westminster we can make sure Scotland's voice is heard and Scotland's interests are to the fore. And with independence, we can devote all of our energies to making sure Scotland is the best place to do business in Europe – securing high-skilled jobs and ushering in a new golden age of innovation off our shores.

Scotland faces a choice. We can let London take the decisions even if that means those decisions are not in Scotland's best interests, or we can choose to take responsibility ourselves, unleashing our potential and securing our own future. Ultimately that choice is yours.

A new Enlightenment

Our ambition for Scotland is about more than increasing wealth and delivering greater social justice. It is also about developing a growing confidence and creativity – a new time in our national life to match the heights of achievement of the Scottish Enlightenment. Today, in many fields of science and discovery, we remain world leaders. And there is a vibrancy and confidence about culture at all levels across Scotland.

The success of the award-winning play *Black Watch* exemplifies this, with the *New York Times* reporting that it arrived in the US 'like a blazing redeemer . . . a necessary reminder of the transporting power that is unique to theatre. Other narrative forms . . . could tell the story that is told here. But none could summon and deploy the array of artistic tools that is used with such mastery and immediacy. Every moment in *Black Watch* seems to bleed from the previous one in an uninterrupted river of sensations.' In our new National Theatre of Scotland there is so much to make us proud.

One of the most famous books about the Scottish Enlightenment is Arthur Herman's *How the Scots Invented the Modern World*. We are fortunate that in so many ways this is still the case. Across Scotland so much good work is being done and the SNP has no doubt there is much more we can achieve. We are still shaping the future. Thanks to Scottish scientists, we could see video screens no thicker than the page of a book. The University of the West of Scotland's Thin Film Centre is the only one of its kind in the UK, and its most recent project will result in flexible, unbreakable electronic display screens as thin as paper. This will revolutionise the way we interact with digital media in our everyday lives.

And as the nation that discovered penicillin and the MRI scan, we are still curing and treating the modern world. Thanks to researchers in Glasgow there will be more effective treatments for leukaemia. The Paul O'Gorman Leukaemia Research Centre at Glasgow University has helped pioneer Glivec, the so-called 'miracle drug' for the treatment of chronic myeloid leukaemia, and it is working to develop new ways of stopping the disease altogether. And in Aberdeen, researchers have developed a unique treatment which targets the so-called 'Alzheimer tangles' that destroy nerve cells critical for memory. This is the first ever drug to act on the tangles, and is a hugely significant development in the treatment of Alzheimer's.

Scotland has long been a leader in scientific advances and is ranked second in the world behind only Switzerland and ahead of the USA in terms of the impact of the research we produce – we punch well above our weight.

And we are working hard to ensure that we produce a new

generation of creative, inventive Scots. We are introducing a Scottish Science Baccalaureate to support science education and investing more to support science teaching and create science clubs in our schools. We are determined to showcase the best of Scottish science, culture and thinking to the world and ensure the most fertile environment for the next generation of Scottish artists and innovators.

'Great Scottish minds and innovation' was one of the strands of our Homecoming Scotland celebration in 2009, as we invited people of Scottish descent, or Scottish affinity, to help us mark the 250th anniversary of the birth of Robert Burns, a Scot of truly global significance. Homecoming was a success at bringing the world to Scotland – delivering a much needed tourism boost at a time of global economic pressure – and now our task in the years that follow is to take Scotland to the world.

That is the driving force behind the Expo Fund. This was one of our key manifesto commitments for promoting and supporting Scottish culture. It has already allowed a range of diverse works to be commissioned, including Scottish Opera's production of Smetana's *The Two Widows*, premiered at the Edinburgh International Festival, sculpture for the Art Festival by renowned Scots artist Jim Lambie, the Winter Festival's outdoor Feet First event and the Made in Scotland series at last year's Edinburgh Festivals, and in October 2009 it sent fourteen Scottish authors to Canada to attend the International Festival of Authors in Toronto.

Creativity is an essential part of the modern economy and society we want to emerge here in Scotland. The creative industries are an important part of that vision, with centres of excellence, for example in the University of Abertay, ensuring Scotland is at the forefront of this growing sector. And we will be leading the campaign to persuade the government in London to give this industry of the future the same tax breaks as in other similar nations, so existing jobs are kept in Scotland and more jobs come to Scotland.

Of course cultural expression and scientific creativity often go hand in hand. At Heriot-Watt University researchers are developing coverings and textiles that can change colour and pattern, using dyes that respond to temperature change to produce a varied and varying spectrum. These changes can be triggered by touch through body temperature. Or, through integrated circuitry, the materials can be programmed to transform themselves when they reach activation temperatures. These visually exciting textiles could be the future of interior design – and they are made in Scotland.

Much is being done and so much more can be achieved. The SNP wants to harness all this Scottish potential through our work in government and by promoting Scottish interests. And of course we believe that it is with independence that economically, culturally and scientifically, Scotland will truly flourish.

Independence

The SNP cares about success for the people of Scotland. That is why we are passionate about independence and equality for our nation.

In his introduction to the Scottish Government's White Paper *Your Scotland, Your Voice* (November 2009), Alex Salmond said: 'Two things are clear. First, that there is a demand in Scotland to consider and debate our national future. Second, that the current arrangements do not meet the ambitions of our nation. Ten years on from devolution, almost all agree that it is time to expand the responsibilities of our parliament.'

The SNP wants Scotland to enjoy the full responsibilities of independence. We believe the 300-year-old political union is no longer fit for purpose. It was never designed for the 21st-century world. It's time for a new partnership on these isles – a social union that ensures Scotland and England are equal nations, friends and partners, both free to make our own choices. Independence will create a new, more appropriate relationship on these isles. It will allow us to work together when that makes sense, and enable Scotland to take all necessary decisions to build prosperity and make the most of the many opportunities that exist for our nation.

Success for Scotland

Scotland can be more successful. That is the simple truth that sits at the heart of our ambition to deliver independence for our nation. Independence is of course the natural state for nations like our own. By taking on more responsibility for our own future, and building a new partnership with the other nations of the UK and the EU, Scotland can make the most of our people, talent and potential to become one of the big success stories of the twenty-first century.

We have a modern, diverse, knowledge-based economy with a total annual economic output of over £100 billion. As we've already mentioned, this includes important sectors such as the service sector, manufacturing, engineering, energy (including oil and gas), financial services, food and drink (including agriculture and fisheries), tourism, the creative industries and life sciences. Our nation has a strong academic base, with four of our universities in the world's top 150. For these reasons, we should be matching the success of similar independent nations.

IMF estimates show that despite the downturn, and the claims of some, the wealth per person in Iceland, Ireland and Norway, nations with a similar population to Scotland, is not only larger than the UK's but that the gap between those nations and the UK will actually increase over the next five years (see Table 1).

With independence Scotland will be free to flourish and grow. We can give our nation a competitive edge.

Table 1: Gross domestic product per capita based on purchasing power parity

	2009	2010	2011	2012	2013	2014
Iceland	35,757,53	35,484.96	36,798.59	38,625.92	40,752.46	43,127.06
Ireland	39,382.54	38,253.28	38,745.75	39,925.78	41,404.23	42,947.46
Norway	52,796.52	52,854.69	53,761.22	55,139.71	56,830.33	58,610.09
UK	35,286.03	34,881.40	35,401.91	36,540.60	37,838.03	38,807.83

Source: World Economic Outlook Database, April 2009

Scotching some independence myths

There has always been a debate about Scotland's financial position. The most recent Government Expenditure and Revenue Scotland (GERS) figures demonstrate that Scottish public finances ran current budget surpluses in each of the three years to 2007/8 (see Table 2). In comparison the UK ran a budget deficit in each of those years. This counters the claims of some that Scotland is subsidised by the UK. The opposite is the case and the Scotland that emerges into independence will be in a stronger financial position than the UK.

Table 2: Balance on current budget, £ billions

	2005/6	2006/7	2007/8	Cumulative total
Scotland	1.0	1.1	0.2	2.3
UK	-13.9	-5.0	-5.1	-24.0

Similarly, some people question how Scotland can afford to pay welfare support and pensions. However, in both 2006/7 and 2007/8, a smaller percentage of government revenue was spent on welfare in Scotland than in the United Kingdom. Spending on social protection accounted for 34 per cent of total government revenue in the UK and 33 per cent in Scotland. This makes clear that we in Scotland are in a better position to pay our pensions and welfare support than the UK as a whole.

Others have asked how an independent Scotland could afford its share of the growing UK debt. First, over the past couple of years, tax revenues in Scotland have been more buoyant than in the UK as a whole. So as the UK has been building up debt, Scotland has been in a relatively stronger position. Second, Scotland would have the collateral to cover future debt and would be in a more advantageous position than the UK and most other western nations. Remaining UK oil and gas reserves have an estimated wholesale value of up to £1.1 trillion. This compares to an accumulated UK debt of £799 billion. A per capita share of UK debt allocated to Scotland would be £68 billion compared to a potential wholesale value of Scotland's oil and gas of almost £1 trillion and resulting government revenues in the hundreds of millions.

People also question how Scotland could have dealt with the bail-out of the banks. There were some large numbers talked about at the time but we now know from the UK government's Pre-Budget Report of December 2009 that the bank bail-outs are expected to cost the Treasury £10 billion for all banks across the UK, not just Scotland. The same report told us that oil revenues are going to be £10 billion higher than expected over the next five years – totalling £50 billion (see Table 3). Again, with 90 per cent of oil revenues falling to Scotland, it is clear that Scotland, like every other EU nation, would have been well able to support its banks.

Finally, some believe that Scotland gets a fair financial benefit from UK defence spending and from being part of wider UK defence arrangements. They even suggest that independence would threaten Scottish defence jobs. Nothing could be further from the

Table 3: Forecast oil & gas revenues, £ billion

	Pre-Budget Report 2009	Budget 2009
2009/10	7.0	6.9
2010/11	8.4	6.6
2011/12	8.6	6.6
2012/13	9.3	6.3
2013/14	8.7	6.1
2014/15	8.0	n/a
TOTAL	50.0	32.5

Source: HM Treasury

truth. The current arrangements mean that Scotland is pulled into conflicts that people here don't support, for example the Iraq War. They also see Scotland as the site of the UK's nuclear weapons, making us the biggest nuclear target on these isles. And on the financial side, Ministry of Defence figures show that Scotland receives a proportionately lower direct economic benefit from UK government defence spending than it might expect. Between 2002 and 2007 there was a £4.3 billion defence underspend in Scotland, compared to our population share of UK defence spending. Defence employment in Scotland, for both service and civilian MoD personnel, has fallen from 24,200 in 1997 to 17,900 in 2009, a proportionately larger fall than in the United Kingdom as a whole. Other similar nations, for example in Scandinavia, have more defence employment and bigger defence sectors and are free to decide whether or not to send their young men and women into conflicts overseas. Scotland is not well served by the Union in comparison to these similar nations.

Economic choice, economic opportunity

For the London parties, the arguments about independence are based on myths – their assertion is that Scotland is somehow uniquely incapable of managing its own affairs well. But as we have seen above, the myths that are peddled are easily swept aside by the facts. Rather than the recession being an argument against independence, it more than anything makes our case.

Scotland has suffered the biggest downturn in living memory as part of the Union. The UK entered the recession first and is one of the last nations to emerge. And while others are acting now to stimulate their economies, the UK's financial plans mean that spending cuts will actually take 1 per cent off economic growth this coming year.

Table 4 shows that the UK is the only major economy that is not acting to stimulate growth this year, and that is costing Scotland dear. We are being held back from recovery because we are not able to take the actions that other countries know are necessary to ensure the most effective recovery.

The Pre-Budget Report also confirmed that the UK government was reducing Scottish spending by £800 million, including its decision not to accelerate £300 million of infrastructure spending into this year to support jobs and recovery. This decision will cost

Table 4: Discretionary stimulus measures in the G7 countries (% of GDP)

	2009	2010
Canada	1.9	1.7
France	0.7	0.8
Germany	1.6	2.0
Italy	0.2	0.1
Japan	2.4	1.8
United Kingdom	1.6	0.0
United States	2.0	1.8
G20 – unweighted average	1.5	1.1

Source: IMF, 'The State of the Public Finances Cross-Country Fiscal Monitor', November 2009

5,000 jobs in Scotland. At a time when Scotland was contributing billions in oil revenues, the UK was unwilling to pass back just £300 million. As an independent country, Scotland would have been able to make very different budget choices. Faced with a revenue increase, we would not have to cut back on investment in infrastructure or the jobs that that would create. This is a clear and simple illustration of the difference independence would make. It is why we need the full responsibilities of independence to ensure that Scotland does once again flourish.

For us the arguments for independence are based on hope and aspiration – a belief in Scotland's ability to prosper when we take decisions for ourselves. They are grounded in the reality of independence enjoyed by nations big and small all around the world. These nations offer proof positive that independence is the natural choice. No country that has moved to independence has ever sought to give up that independence. Does anyone believe that Ireland or Norway would rather have the important decisions taken for them by London or Stockholm?

We are so confident independence is the best choice for Scotland's future that we want your voice to be heard on this issue in a referendum.

Alex Salmond on independence in the modern world, April 2009

In Scotland, as we consider our nation's future, we must consider changes in the nature and utility of political independence – not just in our nation but globally.

This is discussed by Professor Tom Nairn and others like him, who see the emergence of a 'New Deal' at the heart of globalisation. In this environment smaller nations are now exercising their natural strengths: flexibility, speed

of decision-making, defined national interests and a clear
economic strategy.

The European Union has permanently changed the
nature of Scottish membership of the United Kingdom.
Indeed it fatally weakened the pro-Union case.

An independent Scotland would remain a committed
member of the EU. And we would be active and positive at
other levels of governance, not least in the United Nations.
Because while each of these bodies requires the sharing of
sovereignty, there are large and visible benefits to collective
international action.

And among the nations of the British Islands, whether
members of the Union or independent, there will always be
friendship, respect, trust and partnership.

For example, the British–Irish Council brings together all
the heads of government of the British Isles and provides
an excellent forum for cross-border partnership. When
we met in Dublin earlier this year we agreed to extend co-
operation on several issues of shared concern, including
justice, energy and climate change. And I know that this
close and constructive partnership, which unites all the
nations of our isles, will provide the basis for sustained co-
operation and achievement.

Taken together, these examples all show that the
nature of political independence has changed. They show
that today, although the sovereignty of each nation has
only one home, it has many houses; that the place of
Scotland – like any independent nation – is changing in the
modern world.

The referendum

The SNP believes that the people of Scotland should have their say on the future of our nation in a referendum on extending the responsibilities of the Scottish Parliament. That is why we are taking forward a Referendum Bill in the Scottish Parliament this year. At the moment the London parties are opposed to a referendum, but we question why they don't trust the people.

We recognise that a majority of Scots want the Scottish Parliament to be able to do more and so opposition parties will have the opportunity during the bill's passage to bring forward a proposal to include further devolution in the referendum. The referendum can therefore offer multiple options, allowing people to have their say on the status quo and on extending the responsibilities of the parliament to allow for maximum devolution or to allow Scotland to become independent.

The referendum will be held on similar lines to the 1997 devolution vote, but with additional provisions to govern the scrutiny of the process through an independent commission, the levels of finance that can be spent during the campaign, and the mechanism for the count. The arrangements will meet or exceed the best international practice.

The Scottish Parliament will be invited to pass the Referendum Bill legislation so the people can have their say. The precise form of the question will be contained in the bill and will require the whole parliament to approve it.

All referenda in the UK are advisory (with the exception of the 1979 'rigged referendum' on devolution, which, by means of the notorious 40 per cent rule, was heavily weighted against a 'yes' vote by the then Labour government). But it is inconceivable that any UK government would ignore the clear wish of the Scottish people to move to independence. That would flout international law and the very principles of democracy.

If the people of Scotland decided against the independence option, then the government would accept that this was a generational choice. We would not seek to introduce another Referendum Bill within such a timescale.

Some people say we can't afford the cost of a democratic vote. The final cost will be published in the financial resolution accompanying the bill but will be broadly in line with the cost of other referenda held by Westminster – a one-off cost of less than £2 for every Scot. However, a successful outcome would mean that every year we would save the £9 million cost of the House of Lords, the £8 million cost of the Secretary of State for Scotland and the £32 million cost of the House of Commons. We think the people's voice should be heard. Instead of spending our money every year on the House of Lords – and on the weapons of mass destruction which are stored on the Clyde – we can give the people their say.

The same people also argue that the timing of the referendum is wrong. However, Labour are proposing their own referendum, on proportional representation, early in a new parliament at Westminster and they will be taking the legislation through the House of Commons at the same time as the Referendum Bill goes through the Scottish Parliament.

It seems strange that Labour should argue for a referendum on proportional representation for the UK in 2010 but say the people of Scotland can't have their say on more responsibilities for the Scottish Parliament. And Labour, Tory and Liberal Democrat politicians all support a referendum in Wales on new powers for the Welsh Assembly. We think that is hypocritical.

The latest polls tell us that 75 per cent of Scots think we should have a referendum on independence and over two-thirds agree that our parliament should be able to do more. People recognise that the more responsibilities we have here in Scotland the better equipped we are to respond to the downturn and deliver stronger recovery and growth. The Scottish Parliament should have the tools it needs to make Scotland more successful.

The time is therefore right and the passage of the bill can bring closer a Scottish Parliament that can fully and effectively tackle unemployment and financial recovery.

We believe the dividend of independence will transform this country. However, the decision must be yours. Through a referendum, it is right that the people of Scotland are heard.

Alex Salmond on the sovereignty of the people, University of Virginia, April 2008

Scotland has yet to resolve as a nation what collective decision we want to make about our constitutional status. Where America has chosen independence, we have yet to follow. But if we follow your lead, and I have no doubt that we can and we will, in that historic journey, we would have no better guide than Thomas Jefferson.

Thomas Jefferson and all of the Founding Fathers were aware that in creating American democracy, they were also elaborating basic and enduring principles to guide all nations. Indeed, Abraham Lincoln himself said that 'the principles of Jefferson are the axioms of a free society'. So let me focus on three of his founding principles.

First, from which all else follows, the people are sovereign. Or, as Jefferson put it, 'it is the people, to whom all authority belongs'. This is a principle with which many peoples, including those of the United Kingdom, would find it difficult to disagree. But it is our willingness to accept the full implications of this principle – that the people are sovereign – which is the true test of our commitment to democracy. This is a test that even today some in the United Kingdom are not able to pass.

There are supporters of the present Union both in Scotland and elsewhere in the United Kingdom who are unwilling to even consider the question of Scottish independence. And most extraordinarily of all, there are politicians who consider that it is they and not the people of Scotland who should arbitrate and determine the nature of further constitutional change in Scotland.

We need not pause for long to consider what Thomas Jefferson would have made of this state of affairs. Because even the briefest consideration of the second founding principle on which I wish to draw puts the answer plainly.

Jefferson wrote: 'Every nation has a right to govern itself internally under what forms it pleases, and to change these forms at its own will.' This is the basis on which the United States first asserted its right to self-government. It remains one of your fundamental democratic principles. And it is the guiding principle for the debate on Scotland's future.

Thus, when the people of Scotland consider their place in the world and debate our constitutional future, the proper means to exercise this sovereignty is through a referendum.

The vast majority of people in Scotland wish a referendum. That is their right. My wish is for an independent Scotland. Others disagree. I respect that divergence as the very stuff of politics – the clash of ideas and concepts and principles. But what I absolutely demand is that the decision is made not by Parliament alone but rather with the clear direction of the people expressed in a referendum.

I think I know which side of the argument Thomas Jefferson would have supported.

For Jefferson enshrined a vital third constitutional principle. He demanded that, having settled on a constitution, the people of a nation remain free for all time to amend it and to renew their form of government. This is a permanent right, irrespective of whether a nation's circumstances – whether internal or external – change. This is our right and this is the time for the people of Scotland to consider our nation's future.

Focus on economic recovery

Since the start of the recession, the SNP has taken forward an Economic Recovery Plan to ensure that every area of government activity supports our commitments to deliver economic recovery and long-term sustainable growth. Our plan has three key elements:

- Supporting jobs and our communities
- Strengthening Scotland's education and skills
- Investing in innovation and the industries of the future.

Throughout this chapter we will explore the actions we have taken so far and the next steps we plan to ensure Scotland emerges strong and confident from the recession. There are real pressures on families and individuals, with people concerned in particular about jobs.

The downturn has made our action on sustainable economic growth even more critical. As confidence returns there remain challenges, including tackling unemployment and its damaging effects. We have learned lessons from previous recessions, where rising long-term unemployment created lasting damage to Scotland's communities that carried across generations, and we are determined that this time no community will be left behind.

By working together here with local government and other bodies, we have managed to ensure that unemployment in Scotland has been lower than in the rest of the UK in every month the SNP has been in office. This compares to just ten months out of ninety-six under the previous administration. Similarly, employment has been higher in Scotland than in the rest of the UK in every month the SNP has been in office. Some would like to suggest that the recession is hitting Scotland harder than elsewhere, but in the important measure of employment that is clearly not the case. For example, in recent months Sainsbury's have announced the creation of 1,300 jobs in Scotland by the end of 2010, Scottish and Southern Energy have confirmed 250 new high-quality jobs (and safeguarded a further seventy) at the £20 million Centre of Engineering Excellence in Glasgow, and Tesco Bank have established their headquarters in Edinburgh as part of their declared plans for 1,750 Scottish jobs.

The SNP is focused on supporting jobs and communities. That means creating and protecting jobs and supporting the people of Scotland through the downturn. The key measures we have introduced are detailed below.

We've reduced the tax burden on businesses and households. The Small Business Bonus removes tens of thousands of small businesses from the burden of business rates. The expansion of the scheme this year has saved the average small business owner £1,400. A survey by the Federation of Small Businesses suggested this had helped 14 per cent of their members survive the downturn, protecting valuable jobs in local communities. In the year ahead we are giving

Scottish business a further £220 million competitive boost, by ensuring that total rates bills are well below the levels elsewhere in the UK. This will support Scottish companies as we emerge from recession and allow them to compete more effectively and create new jobs.

Households have also been helped with the extension of the council tax freeze for a second year in 2009, and the resources are available to freeze council tax again in the year to come. This will save Scottish households £420 million over the three years.

We've accelerated improvements to the planning process to help the right developments go forward more quickly. This includes the launch of a new online planning system, ePlanning, which will make planning in Scotland simpler, faster and more accessible. In the second half of 2009 more than 80 per cent of written planning appeals were dealt with within twelve weeks, compared to 27 per cent in 2008/9 and only 6 per cent in 2007/8. This is a big improvement that will make Scotland a more attractive place for investment and business.

We are directly investing in communities through a £60 million Town Centre Regeneration Fund, which will help local agencies to regenerate their town centres. Communities will also be helped through accelerated spending from the European Structural Funds, the Scottish Rural Development Programme and the European Fisheries Fund.

The second part of our Economic Recovery Plan is to strengthen Scotland's education and skills. A central element is ScotAction, our skills package designed to **support businesses and individuals**. Key parts of the package are the Adopt an Apprentice scheme, which allows apprentices made redundant elsewhere to finish their work and studies, and Safeguard an Apprentice, which provides wage support for businesses if they keep an apprentice employed. We've provided an extra £16 million to support an additional 7,800 apprentices this year.

We are also **increasing support for people facing redundancy** with the strengthening of the Partnership Action for Continuing Employment (PACE) initiative to help those businesses and individuals faced with job losses. PACE has allowed many people to find new jobs or training.

And we are **strengthening education for young people** through the 16+ Learning Choices scheme to offer a place of learning to every young person as they reach the school-leaving age. This initiative is a crucial part of recovery, because it is only through a highly educated and skilled population that Scotland will truly flourish in the future. We'll explore some of these in more detail over the next few chapters.

The third part of the plan covers investment in innovation and the industries of the future. We are **increasing incentives for business to use and pursue innovation**, with Scottish Enterprise's research and development grant programme attracting over £100 million of private sector investment into research projects. And the £10 million Saltire Prize has been launched to provide the largest innovation prize for marine renewables, putting Scotland at the forefront of this emerging and potentially planet-saving technology.

Research and innovation are crucial to our emerging industries, which will be the major employers of the future. We are determined to support companies with the potential for growth. By **establishing a Scottish Investment Bank**, with initial funds of £150 million, we can support innovative high-growth potential businesses.

Scotland has huge strengths and enormous potential and that must be translated into greater prosperity and opportunity for hard-working families and individuals in communities across our nation. The SNP is focused on recovery as a starting point, and through our Economic Recovery Plan, we are not only working to protect employment and support business today, we are also laying the ground work for a more successful and prosperous future.

The impact of many of these initiatives will be felt throughout this year, with some of the biggest steps, including the new tax advantage for Scottish business starting in April 2010. This will help Scottish companies grow just as we need them to deliver new jobs and new opportunities.

John Swinney sets out initiatives as part of Scotland's Economic Recovery Plan, October 2009

It is now more than a year since the Scottish Government first took action to support the Scottish economy through the downturn. We have taken measures to ensure that accelerated capital expenditure at national and local levels has supported direct employment.

We are spending almost £3.8 billion on capital investment this financial year, which includes the acceleration of £293 million. That spending is providing a significant stimulus to the construction industry, and it will ultimately support nearly 37,000 jobs in the construction sector alone. The accelerated capital expenditure, which is a proportion of that, has been enormously valuable in supporting economic recovery.

In addition to the support for capital expenditure and the acceleration of many investments through the European Social Fund and the European Regional Development Fund, the government's economic strategy rests on capitalising on Scotland's greatest comparative advantage: its people.

A healthy, well-trained and well-educated workforce is

pivotal to shaping the long-term success of our economy. The ScotAction programme, which the Cabinet Secretary for Education and Lifelong Learning launched, represents a major package of measures to meet the challenges and help individuals and employers. With an extra £16 million, we have funded an additional 7,800 apprentices in this financial year, which represents a 73 per cent increase on normal funded apprenticeship places.

Yesterday it was announced that a successful bid for European Social Fund moneys means that we can further extend the apprenticeship scheme. The cabinet secretary today visited one of the companies that will take part in the new scheme to provide a golden hello of £2,000 to 16–19-year-olds in the manufacturing, textiles, food and drink and energy sectors. The approach will provide much-needed assistance.

The government's economic recovery plan also focuses on investing in innovation and industries of the future. There is a great opportunity for us in the context of what we can achieve in the renewables sector and as part of the creation of a low-carbon economy. Scotland's future rests on the development of innovative technology and we are determined to ensure that we deploy our resources and provide the support that is necessary to ensure that we can create tens of thousands of green jobs during the next decade in diverse generation systems and in energy management, energy efficiency, renewables, biomass and recycling.

The government is focused on ensuring that we deliver economic recovery in Scotland. We must operate in a challenging climate. We pledge our commitment to working with all aspects of the Scottish economy to deliver the prosperity that our people require.

Value for your money

A key part of our approach, alongside our actions to support economic recovery, is to make sure maximum resources are directed towards the frontline. That means less being spent on civil service bureaucracy and the public sector sharing in the belt-tightening that we are all facing.

This has been an important part of our agenda since we took office in May 2007. One of our first acts was to reduce the number of ministers and political advisers and cut by one-third the number of government departments. In March that year John Swinney MSP set out our approach to efficient government:

> The SNP will deliver smaller government. Our government will take a series of sensible steps to deliver more effective government including fewer departments and the abolition or merger of a number of quangos. We will have fewer ministers than the current Scottish Executive, with a Cabinet of six providing the strategic leadership and direction to our administration.
>
> It is our determination that the benefits of these measures are felt fully by families and communities across Scotland. That's why our smaller, more efficient Scottish government will prioritise the frontline.

In government we have set targets for efficiency savings which will deliver a 6 per cent efficiency gain of £1.6 billion over the coming year. Our efficiency programme will see this money available to invest in the public services that matter and it will allow us to support families and businesses with lower local tax.

As a result of SNP action in government we are saving £160 million through smarter public procurement, £82 million by managing our assets better and £12 million through the sharing of back office services across the public sector.

We are looking to do more, with the number of quangos due to be cut by 25 per cent by 2011, bringing an additional saving of £40 million each year – money that can be spent on our hospitals and schools. And in the year ahead we will cut the central government salary bill by more than 4 per cent and reduce the amount we spend on marketing and advertising by 50 per cent.

These are the right choices – less government waste, more staff employed to deliver frontline services, and the people of Scotland able to keep more of the money they earn to ease some of the pressures on family budgets.

We have already announced a freeze on senior civil service salaries (those over £58,000) and will look to extend this throughout the public sector. And because we want to lead by example, SNP ministers are taking a pay freeze this year on their ministerial salaries. We believe those who earn most in the public sector should play their part in these difficult times, while those on the lowest wages continue to get pay increases.

We reject Conservative plans for a wage freeze across the public sector, which would hit 99 per cent of police officers, 96 per cent of teachers and 97 per cent of nurses, midwives and paramedics. Most Scots don't believe these hard-working public servants should be hit when Tory plans would see tax gains for millionaires. And we also reject the Liberal Democrats' five-year wage plans, which would see newly qualified police officers and teachers lose over £3,000 and newly qualified nurses £2,600. These are the wrong people to be paying for the recession.

The SNP has responsibility for only part of Scotland's public sector. If we are going to secure the best deal for people in Scotland our approach needs to be replicated at Westminster. That's why we need Scottish MPs in the House of Commons making sure that the UK delivers a fair deal and the right deal for Scotland.

Employment and skills

Scotland knows to its cost what happens when a government fails to invest in skills. Our towns and cities still bear the scars of the recessions of the 1980s and 1990s when London governments failed to invest and instead stood by as a generation saw their job prospects destroyed. Scotland must now prioritise skills and training so we can give people the chance they need to be successful in the jobs market.

Scotland's greatest asset is its people. We are working to build a self-confident, outward-looking Scotland – an ambitious nation with opportunities for everyone to make the most of their potential and make a positive contribution to Scotland's success. Investing in our people's skills, ensuring that those skills contribute as much as possible to sustainable economic growth, is central to unlocking this more prosperous future. The SNP will not allow another 'lost generation' to be created.

A smarter Scotland is at the heart of everything we want to achieve for this country. We can build a Scotland that is wealthier and fairer, one that is healthier, safer, stronger and greener, only if people are equipped with the skills, expertise and knowledge for success.

We have made higher education at college and university more accessible to people on low incomes by introducing Individual Learning Accounts 500 – an annual grant of £500 towards study for up to 20,000 students a year. This is on top of our Individual Learning Accounts 200, whereby people can take part in short, flexible pieces of work-focused training. We have extended these to an extra 250,000 people – covering nearly half the adult workforce. The recession has made this ambition all the more important and through our skills programme, ScotAction, we are helping people get jobs, helping them stay in jobs and helping them move between jobs.

While we are helping those in work, we are also providing support for those facing redundancy by helping them move straight into alternative employment.

When jobs are on the line, we know it is critical to get co-ordinated and coherent support in place. Our PACE teams bring together all the public bodies into one team to ensure a swift and effective approach. People at risk of redundancy get tailored help and support to ensure they can develop the skills they need to find new work. Companies of all sizes and all sectors have received this help, supporting thousands of people to quickly find new jobs.

Colleges play a critical role in delivering the skills people need in a recession. They can quickly and flexibly provide the training that makes people attractive to employers. That's why we have announced an additional £28 million so that Scotland's colleges can provide the courses people need to get the skills employers are looking for.

Just one example can be seen in Forth Valley College in Falkirk, where engineers – some made redundant from manufacturing companies – are starting the transformation programme, learning new skills for the oil and gas sector with Opito, the oil and gas academy. It is schemes like this that can make a real difference both to individuals and to companies, who get access to highly skilled workers.

We are learning the lessons of the past and working to make sure the right support is there when jobs are on the line. We have recognised that it is vital to have quick access to training and the Training for Work programme is now available after just three months' unemployment rather than six. And, because we know the longer people are out of work the harder it is to get back into work, those people under threat of redundancy can now access the training scheme during the ninety-day redundancy notification period.

This comes on top of our Apprenticeship Guarantee, which gives £2,000 to every employer who agrees to take on a redundant apprentice, allowing them to complete their training. That is a unique package of support that is keeping apprentices working despite the recession.

Funding, however, is just one part of the solution. Faced with a global downturn, we also have to work more creatively.

We have created Skills Development Scotland (SDS), bringing together all the main skills and career services into one organisation to ensure they work in a joined-up way. Through SDS, we have put careers advisers in the workplace and linked up with Jobcentres to create as seamless a service as possible. The challenge is to make this work despite the Jobcentre network and employment policy being managed from London. If Scotland had responsibility in these areas, an even better, more integrated service could be delivered – providing more support faster and more effectively to those looking for work. When we need it most, it is frustrating that we can't just make it happen.

Scotland has got the talent, determination and ingenuity to tackle the recession and to reskill for recovery. With a powerful voice at Westminster, the SNP can make sure Scotland's interests are to the fore, Scottish communities aren't forgotten and London does its bit too.

ScotAction: the Scottish Government economic recovery plan, November 2009

We have responded to the economic downturn by reshaping and adapting our skills and training policies, making them more flexible, more accessible and more tailored to the needs of individuals and businesses. The ScotAction programme is a major package of measures to help those who are unemployed gain employment, to help employers – particularly in key sectors – develop the skills in their workforce that are vital for economic recovery, and to help people facing redundancy find new jobs.

ScotAction: Skills support for those in work

We are already supporting Scottish businesses and individuals through funding of £16 million for an additional 7,800 apprentices in 2009/10. This represents an increase of 73 per cent on normal funded apprentice places. Skills Development Scotland has now contracted for all of the additional 7,800 apprentices. They include:

- 2,000 apprentices for the retail sector
- 1,250 health and social care apprenticeships
- 1,000 apprentices in Glasgow
- 600 management apprentices
- 170 apprenticeship places for early years and childcare.

We have identified some key sectors for growth in the Scottish economy and are specifically boosting apprenticeships in these sectors to ensure businesses and individuals are equipped with the skills to respond rapidly to an upturn in the economy. Among the 7,800 new apprenticeships we have allocated:

- 500 in the hospitality and tourism sector
- 460 in financial and business services
- 410 in the food and drink industry
- 100 in home energy and efficiency
- 50 in the creative industries.

As part of ScotAction, our 2 for 1: Innovate with an Apprentice initiative supports the development of technician skills to boost the future growth of the life sciences sector. Through the initiative, life science employers receive financial assistance to recruit two apprentices for the cost of one, with the Scottish Government covering the wage costs for the second apprentice during the course of their training.

Higher and further education

Scotland has world-leading colleges and universities. They are a crucial part of the success of our nation and our economy.

That is a source of great pride, but Scotland can also take pride in our national approach to access to higher and further education. We believe that access to colleges and universities – to the learning that leads to greater success in life – should be based on the ability to learn, not the ability to pay. That is the Scottish tradition.

The SNP abolished the back-door tuition fees imposed by the previous Labour–Liberal administration, benefiting 50,000 students immediately, and replaced expensive, discredited student loans with grants for thousands more.

The Graduate Endowment saddled newly qualified graduates with thousands of pounds of debt and deterred too many from less well-off backgrounds from ever going to college or university. Uniquely in the UK, new graduates in Scotland are no longer faced with this burden. While the rest of the UK debates by how much fees will increase, in Scotland, we have held to the fundamental principle that education is a right, not a privilege.

The recession has meant that helping students before they graduate has also become a priority. We know that the downturn has made it harder for students to get the kind of part-time and vocational work that supplements many incomes. The tight jobs market hit just as the credit crunch made it harder and more expensive for students to get bank credit.

Students themselves told us that graduate debt remains an issue but they also told us that in these tough economic times many were facing a stark choice between paying the rent and continuing their studies. The SNP listened and recognised that more help for hard-pressed students had to be made a priority.

To help the hardest hit, we have increased the hardship fund by more than 17 per cent to £16.44 million. To help part-time students – who are often studying to improve their skills and job chances – we have invested £38 million in a new £500 grant, which will move up to 20,000 students a year from loans to grants.

As the recession has bitten, we have gone further. To help single parents studying to improve their own life chances – and those of their children – we have announced that £2 million will be provided to support childcare, and, for the first time, we are making a grant available to independent students. In the midst of the recession, many independent students are studying to get back into the jobs market and are taking a course while also supporting their own families. To help, we will provide a new grant of up to £1,000, benefiting an estimated 14,000 students of all ages who were previously solely reliant on loans.

In the colleges, the impact of the recession on students' finances was no less acute. That's why, through the Scottish Funding Council, the total allocated to further education student support this year will amount to £90.9 million, nearly 10 per cent more than last year and nearly 22 per cent up on the level we inherited from the Labour–Liberal administration.

This help has freed thousands from the fear of dropping out through lack of financial means. When we announced our plans, Liam Burns, NUS Scotland president, said: 'This is great news for students. The government have shown themselves to be responsive, flexible and genuinely working with, and for, students.'

We have done all this while funding our world-class colleges and universities to a greater level than ever before. By increasing funding and ensuring it is comparable to the rest of the UK, we have been able to ensure education is based on the ability to learn and not the ability to pay.

As a result, we have successfully resisted pressure to introduce tuition fees, with the universities themselves acknowledging they are not needed. When asked whether student fees should be introduced in Scotland, Professor Steve Smith, president of Universities UK, speaking at their annual conference in Edinburgh last September, said: 'The issue is almost completely irrelevant in Scotland. It's not something we are thinking about. Because the funding level is roughly comparable with England's it seems to me there is no issue.'

Through the Scottish Funding Council, a total of £1.14 billion has been allocated to higher education for 2009/10 and we plan a further increase in university funding of just over £35 million next year and £45 million in college funding. As result, a greater proportion of the Scottish Government's budget will go to higher education under the SNP government than it ever received under the old Labour–Liberal administration. As Universities Scotland – the representative body for Scottish institutions – said when we announced our spending plans: 'This is a good day for us . . . this budget puts universities right at the heart of the Scottish Government's economic recovery strategy. Universities will respond by delivering real impact with this investment. The message that is being sent out is support for the university sector.'

We are committed to this funding because higher and further education lies at the heart of our economic strategy. We have fashioned a new partnership with our universities, working together to deliver the skills and research the economy needs. The success of our universities can be seen in the world class research pouring from our institutions, with the most recent UK-wide assessment rating 15 per cent of Scottish-based researchers as 'world-leading'.

We have made universities the seventh sector of the economy, giving it parity of esteem with the other major economic sectors for the first time. That means the depth of expertise and knowledge in our universities is being harnessed to boost economic growth for all. Scotland's strength in research and our academic excellence provide firm foundations we can build on for even greater prosperity in the future.

Scotland has got what it takes to remain at the top in key areas of global research and learning. The SNP is determined to keep our university education world-class and based on ability to learn, not ability to pay. With a powerful voice at Westminster, the SNP can speak up for Scotland. We can speak up for our students, lecturers and staff.

Alex Salmond on Scotland's greatest invention – universal education, April 2008

We know Scotland's proud record of invention and our huge contribution, through the Enlightenment, in the development of the ideas that form the foundation of our modern world.

When I was at school I wasn't taught much or indeed any Scottish history, but I did learn that we had invented lots of stuff – television, penicillin, the fax machine, even the bicycle! But no one ever told me why Scots were able to invent so much.

It was because of our greatest invention of all – universal education. Without that Scottish innovation James Watt would never have invented the steam engine, Adam Smith would not be the father of economics and Robert Burns would have blushed unseen with his sweetness wasted on the desert air.

We should be proud to be the party which has reintroduced free education. Free education is back – for all Scots and in all parts of Scotland.

Early years and school education

The SNP is working hard to deliver new opportunities for young Scots. We want to remove the barriers that hold young people back, whether in education or in life. We believe a nation with the wealth and resources of Scotland should be able to deliver the opportunities that allow pupils to succeed and our economy to prosper.

To deliver on that belief, we are focusing our efforts on the issues that impact most on many of the youngest in our society. Whether those challenges are family unemployment, poor parenting skills or parental drug use, we are reshaping the way in which we approach the early years of life, insisting that crisis intervention is not enough; early intervention before any crisis is reached is the way to make a real difference. As a society, by tackling problems before they become crises, we can free our young people from the pattern of underachievement that has blighted too many of our communities – we can help unleash their potential. This is a job not just for government, but for all of us.

We have launched the Play, Talk, Read campaign, giving parents the tools they need to improve their parenting skills and providing additional support so they can give their children the best possible start in life and learning. We are bringing forward reforms to children's hearings to make sure Scotland's unique welfare-based system is fit for the modern world, and we are working with local government to provide better support for foster and kinship carers. To get our youngest children off to the very best start in their education, we are increasing nursery entitlement, delivering more pre-school education in every community in Scotland.

In primary school, we have extended free school meals to an extra 44,000 pupils from hard-pressed families in receipt of maximum child tax credit and maximum working tax credit. That's practical action to make sure children get the healthy, nutritious meal they need if they are to concentrate in class. And working with local government, we are looking to extend free school meal provision for children in Primary 1 to Primary 3, starting in the most deprived communities.

We want Scotland's education to rival any country's in the world.

As a nation we have a strong reputation for education and Scottish education is generally good, but we want it to be among the best in the world. We are aware of the challenges, but we won't let anyone talk down the good work and effort of Scottish pupils and teachers.

This is not simply a question of more money. Over the last ten years, education budgets have increased by 36 per cent. Now we want to see results improve by a similar amount. We need to take Scottish education to a new level. That's why we are now reforming the education system, starting with a new curriculum designed to raise standards of teaching and learning.

We believe teachers know best how to teach Scotland's pupils. The new curriculum, Curriculum for Excellence, sets out our aims for education and allows our teachers to use their professional expertise to deliver those aims without the overbearing demands of a prescriptive curriculum. For teachers, it builds on excellent practices that bring learning to life. It reaches out to industry and enterprise to bring real life to learning. For young people, it offers the ability to personalise their learning and choice within a broad curriculum. It balances the importance of knowledge and skills. It is designed to nurture successful, effective, confident and responsible young people, ready for whatever the twenty-first century may bring.

To fit with this new approach to learning, we are improving the qualifications system. Pupils will be formally assessed in literacy and numeracy during primary school and, for the first time, will have to take a qualification in secondary school in literacy and numeracy. Standard Grades are being replaced with new national exams, Highers are being updated to ensure they remain the gold standard of Scottish education, and the brightest pupils are being stretched with the introduction of new baccalaureates that will push them further. Taken together, this is a significant updating and upgrading of the qualifications system that will reflect pupils' achievements and give employers a true measure of their skills.

Just as the curriculum is changing, so is the way our teachers learn. For a pupil to get the best education, nothing matters more than the quality of teaching. That's why we are investing in additional training and are reviewing the way in which initial teacher training is undertaken.

No matter how good the teacher, however, they cannot deliver the very best education if their classroom is crumbling. For too long, previous governments invested too little in school buildings, leaving pupils to learn in unsuitable accommodation. We are on track to complete more than 250 school building projects by 2011, taking 160,000 pupils out of sub-standard premises, and we have announced a joint investment with Scotland's councils of a further £1.25 billion. Working with Scotland's councils we have set ourselves the task of wiping out sub-standard accommodation completely.

Our ambition does not stop there. To make the most impact, pupils need one-to-one time with their teacher. We know this is particularly true in the earliest years of primary school when the fundamental building blocks of literacy and numeracy are laid down. We have already achieved the lowest average primary school class sizes on record, but we want to go much further and are working with local councils to reduce class sizes in Primary 1 to Primary 3 to eighteen or fewer. There are more pupils in classes of that size than ever before. But there is more to do. We are committed to making the kind of progress that we know will deliver lasting benefits to pupils' education as they progress through school.

Education is the bedrock on which Scotland's success has always been built. It is the bedrock on which our future personal and national prosperity will rest. The SNP government is laying the foundations of an education system that will deliver that prosperity to all.

Michael Russell MSP, Cabinet Secretary for Education and Life-long Learning, on Scotland's education system, December 2009

As we approach the second decade of this century, we know that our education system works well, but we all agree that we need it to be better if we are to compete with the best in the world. Our job in the chamber is to support it and to help it to do better, and that is the task that I take on with my colleagues.

What is our ambition? It is to have a world-beating education service that draws together pre-schools, schools, colleges and universities, with a commitment to keep moving to achieve the highest standards for those who are within the system.

The evidence shows that this has been a year of successful achievement for pupils and their teachers. Together, they have delivered record exam results. Entries for Highers and Advanced Highers rose by 3.2 per cent and 4.2 per cent respectively, despite falling school rolls. Pass rates at Higher and Advanced Higher level are at a record high. Standard Grade pass rates are at their highest since 2000.

Latest comparisons from the 2006/7 school year show that in Scotland, 69.8 per cent of pupils achieved the equivalent of a GCSE pass in English compared with 60.2 per cent in England, 57 per cent of Scottish pupils achieved a similar standard in a science subject compared with only 51.3 per cent in England, and 48.6 per cent of Scottish pupils achieved that standard in a modern language compared with only 30.9 per cent in England. We can and must keep improving.

> We need to have ambition, we need to focus and we
> need to ensure that we make achievements, but let us
> use the right language. Across the parliament, across the
> sector and across Scotland, there is huge commitment and
> enthusiasm.

Climate change and
the environment

Climate change is the biggest global challenge we face and there is
a broad consensus that urgent action needs to be taken to reduce
greenhouse gas emissions. We also need to adapt to the changes to
our environment that are already taking place. We all have a duty
to face up to the challenges presented by the projected changes
in our environment (see Table 5). We believe that Scotland is
well placed to meet its obligations and take the steps required to
confront climate change. This will have an impact on us all and
affect every area of life. And we also have an opportunity to use
our expertise and technology to help the wider world rise to the
challenge.

Scotland's actions on climate change are world-leading. We know
how important it is to show leadership on this critical issue. The
SNP recognises that Scotland's contribution to global efforts can be
significant. We are uniquely placed to spearhead the development
of low-carbon energy technologies, improved water management

Table 5: Climate projections for Scotland

Rainstorm frequency	By 2080 rainfall events will, on average, be unaffected in north-west Scotland, 25–75% more intense in east Scotland, up to 100% more intense in west Scotland and more than 150% more intense in parts of south-west Scotland.
Sea level rises	Scenarios suggest a net sea level rise for Scotland of 15–28cm by the 2080s, an increase in peak surges and a modest annual average increase in tidal surges and waves due to an increasing frequency of severe winter gales.
Flooding	Changes in rainfall intensity will become more dramatic, increasing the likelihood of flash flooding of Scottish rivers.
Precipitation	By the 2080s, there will be 40–60% less winter snowfall over the Cairngorms.

Source: 'Business Risks of Climate Change to Public Sector Organisations in Scotland' (SNIFFER, 2005)

and greater energy efficiency. And that will mean a major expansion of jobs and economic opportunities.

Achievements and actions

The Scottish Government has set an international example through the Climate Change (Scotland) Act 2009. It has been hailed throughout the globe as the most ambitious piece of legislation anywhere, representing the kind of action needed to ensure that we rise to the challenges and opportunities presented by climate change. The Act leads the world in a number of areas, such as:

- Specifying interim targets of 42 per cent reduction of greenhouse gas emissions by 2020 and 80 per cent by 2050, based on 1990 levels
- The inclusion of all six greenhouse gases identified by the Kyoto Protocol, not just CO_2

- A requirement to report on the emissions implications of the Scottish budget – the first annual carbon budget was produced this year
- A duty to include international aviation and shipping.

Along with the Act the Scottish Government also produced the Climate Change Delivery Plan, which sets out the actions that need to be taken now and in the medium-to-long term to achieve our emissions reductions. We recognise that although our overall contribution to global emissions is small, it is imperative to show leadership and demonstrate that the road to a low-carbon and prosperous future is possible. That is at the heart of our approach to delivering higher levels of sustainable economic growth. We can make Scotland greener and wealthier.

As addressed elsewhere, policies on climate change will have an impact on every aspect of our lives. That is why, as Scotland's government, we are working hard to make the most of our renewable energy potential, improving land management techniques and greening our transport among other things. We are acting in a number of ways to build a more environmentally sustainable Scotland, such as progressing towards a zero-waste society. Recycling rates are increasing and Scotland met its obligations to reduce waste under the 2010 EU Landfill Directive eighteen months ahead of schedule. We have halved supermarket plastic bag use and are looking at ways to improve the recyclability of products to further strengthen these aims. Our zero waste strategy will help cut emissions and preserve precious resources. There are also opportunities as treating waste properly could create an additional 2,000 jobs.

The SNP has realised that we all have a role to play in tackling climate change. That is why we introduced a Climate Challenge Fund, worth £28 million. This fund will help empower local communities to reduce their own carbon footprints, by supporting local low-carbon projects. It is a fund that will help communities meet the challenge of climate change. Action at a community level is often most effective and innovative and we want to unlock that potential so that all of Scotland is working together to meet our national climate change targets.

We recognise that some climate change is unavoidable and we are already witnessing its impact in a number of ways, not least in weather patterns. As Scotland's government we are assessing the likely impact of climate change through our Climate Change Adaptation Framework. One area of particular concern is flooding. In recent times we have seen increased flooding and the devastation it brings to communities and people's lives. As a result, we are making record levels of funding available for flood prevention schemes. We were also the first administration in the UK to put the EC Floods Directive into law with the Flood Risk Management Act 2009. That will help speed up the decision-making process to get flood schemes up and running more quickly, and it will establish a National Flooding Review and subsequently a national flood risk management plan. We understand that flooding will continue to be a major issue and want to work with local authorities and communities to improve flood prevention measures.

Achieving more

While Scotland is implementing the most ambitious climate change targets in the world we lack key areas of competence to be as effective as we would like. Our ambitions are constrained and as a nation we are held back from achieving all we could.

Independence would make it easier to meet our targets by giving us the ability to improve the regulations governing our energy sector, for example, so they are better suited to Scottish needs. It would also give us a stronger voice on the international stage. At the Copenhagen summit Scotland was lauded for taking the action needed. However, ministers in London decided Scotland should not be part of the UK delegation – this was a lost opportunity given that we had such a good story to tell. At a European level too it is vital to have a strong voice seeking action to reduce greenhouse gas emissions as well as other actions such as reducing waste, improving the environmental management of our seas and better land management. A voice for Scotland in international forums would have meant a strong voice for tough action to combat climate change.

Scotland has to wait for decisions taken by the UK in so many areas and this has an impact on our ability to meet our climate change targets. And quite often those decisions, when taken, do not reflect particular Scottish circumstances. We need the ability to green our taxes so that we can reward innovative and environmentally sustainable behaviour and boost our green technologies. For example at present the Exchequer in London receives over £80 million each year in receipts for landfill tax, cash which could help us in our ambitious targets to create a zero waste society. In other areas such as transport, energy and rural management we lack the means to build a greener society. That does not mean acting alone but rather acting in partnership with authorities throughout these islands, Europe and beyond and showing global leadership by our actions.

Scotland has achieved a lot with the responsibilities that we have. However, we could do so much more if we could take more of our own decisions. That would be good for Scotland and great for the planet.

Energy

Scotland is an energy-rich country. The oil and gas industry is a massive contributor to the Scottish economy and the UK Treasury, and our growing low-carbon energy sector has the potential to be every bit as successful. Following the discovery of oil in the 1960s, the North Sea industry became a world leader, allowing for the development of Scottish-based skills, expertise and technology. These have made Scotland a significant global player in the energy industry and Aberdeen is the world's second biggest energy hub.

We are also seeing Scotland emerge as a leader in green energy technologies. Scotland has vast renewable energy resources, with approximately a quarter of the EU's wind and tidal resources and 10 per cent of its wave resources. Scotland has enough renewables potential to power the country at peak demand ten times over. Those resources along with the skills, technology and ambition needed to succeed means that Scotland is well placed to become a leader in renewables technology and expertise and a major exporter of clean green energy. Scotland is also well placed in the development of other low-carbon energy technologies. For example, we have the greatest carbon capture and storage potential in the EU and are well placed to take forward the development of a North Sea electricity grid. We are determined to develop Scotland's comparative advantages in the energy sector to meet the twin global challenges of climate change and energy security.

Achievements so far

Energy is a key sector for the SNP in government and at Westminster and Brussels. We are determined to ensure that the oil and gas and other traditional industries thrive while growing the renewables sector to meet our energy needs and international climate targets. The Scottish Government is responsible for many of the policy-making areas such as planning, promoting renewables, energy efficiency and emergency planning. We are determined to use all of our responsibilities to build our energy sector and ensure it continues to thrive.

A mix of technologies will be required to secure a low-carbon and secure energy future. However, we are clear that nuclear energy has no part to play. Nuclear is unreliable and expensive, with new nuclear power stations around Europe exceeding their budgets and timescales. The expense does not stop there; in July 2008 the Westminster Public Accounts Committee concluded that the nuclear clean-up would cost £73 billion. We would rather see that money invested in our renewable and low-carbon energy technologies, helping us meet our aspiration of decarbonising our electricity sector by 2030.

Scotland has massive renewable resources in onshore and offshore wind, tidal power and wave power. The total has been estimated at 60 gigawatts, enough to power Scotland ten times over. That is a huge resource – much more than Scotland's annual electricity consumption – and has the potential to provide clean green energy for export to the rest of the UK and Europe. We would like to see the development of a North Sea grid so that this electricity can be transported across to the Continent, and we welcome the EU's far-sighted work to make that possible. We can help the whole of Europe meet its renewable energy targets.

The Crown Estate has awarded a series of 'exclusivity agreements' to companies for offshore wind sites around Scotland's shores. These could be worth billions of pounds to the economy, creating tens of thousands of jobs and providing much of our electricity. Rather than an 'energy gap', Scotland very much has an energy opportunity.

The SNP in government has introduced a number of measures to ensure that we can fulfil our renewables potential. The £10 million Saltire Prize is one of the biggest innovation prizes in history. It is Scotland's challenge to the world to push the frontiers of innovation in marine energy and has already had 130 expressions of interest from five continents around the world. National Geographic, the world's largest educational charity, is working with us on this project and they have described the Saltire Prize as a great example of a small nation making a big difference to a global challenge. We also took the difficult decision to replace the Beauly–Denny power line. That will help unlock Scotland's vast green energy resources and help to secure our energy needs as well as export green energy to the rest of Europe.

We are also working with the Energy Technology Partnership (ETP), made up of leading researchers at Scotland's universities, to drive forward research and commercialisation opportunities, building on our recognised expertise in engineering and green energy innovation. The Scottish European Green Energy Centre, based in Aberdeen, will act as a focal point for the development of the sector in Europe, in close collaboration with the ETP. Its main aims will be to support sustainable economic growth and energy targets, foster good practice and promote the internationalisation of green energy research. It will place Scotland at the cutting edge of developments in green energy in Europe.

The SNP recognises the continued importance of the oil and gas industry. It has been calculated that oil and gas have contributed £269 billion to the UK Treasury since 1977. The skills and expertise of its workers have also brought about economic benefits, and international sales from the supply chain amount to £5 billion annually.

Many of the skills that played a pivotal role in developing the oil and gas industry will be needed to ensure the success of our renewables sector. The oil and gas supply chain in Scotland is hugely successful with new opportunities emerging. One area where we can maintain the natural advantage gained through North Sea is the development of carbon capture and storage. The CO_2 storage research study of 2009 whose primary sponsor was the Scottish Government concluded that Scotland has enough capacity to store its CO_2 emissions for 200 years and greater storage potential than Germany, the Netherlands and Denmark combined.

Energy efficiency is also a priority. Greater energy efficiency is one of the most effective ways to bring down bills and emissions. Energy efficiency will play an important role in tackling climate change, fuel poverty and building our economy, and SNP ministers are giving greater emphasis to that through the Energy Efficiency Action plan. In government we have taken a number of important steps already such as:

- The Energy Saving Scotland network of advice centres, providing a one-stop shop on energy efficiency
- Greater co-ordination of our energy efficiency and fuel poverty programmes as recommended by the Fuel Poverty Forum through the Energy Assistance Package
- £15 million Scottish Government funding for a home insulation scheme
- Energy Efficiency Design awards to support innovative measures to improve energy efficiency.

Looking to the future

It is with the normal responsibilities of independence that Scotland could truly fulfil its energy potential and put the policies in place that would help the industry grow more quickly.

The existing approach to energy regulation for access to the grid works against the interests of Scotland's energy industry. The application of locational charging, which levies higher charges on generators located further from the centres of demand, puts Scottish generators, especially renewables, at a disadvantage. By its very nature much of Scotland's renewable energy potential, such as offshore wind in the Moray Firth and tidal power in the Pentland Firth, is located far from population centres and so the generators are penalised under the current regime.

Scottish generators produce 12 per cent of the UK's generation but pay 40 per cent of the transmission costs, £100 million per year more than their proportionate share. This undermines a level playing field and our ability to fulfil our green energy potential. An independent Scotland would have the ability to deliver a fair electricity market that encourages green energy generation rather than penalising it.

With greater responsibilities Scotland would build even closer ties with our partners. The EU is an increasingly important player in the development of green energy and has set ambitious renewable energy targets. Scotland has already surpassed the UK's target and will meet 31 per cent of its electricity demand from renewables by 2011 and 50 per cent by 2020. We want to build on that and, given our resources, we believe that Scotland will be a major exporter of clean green energy in the future. That means working with the EU and other member states in developing the technologies and infrastructure necessary so we can meet these export ambitions. We could create an energy hub in the North Sea, giving Europe the security of supply that it desperately needs. Member states are increasingly working together to deliver their targets and as Europe's green energy hub Scotland should be at the heart of those collaborations.

If Scotland is to meet its energy potential we need to develop the right kind of infrastructure such as ports, network upgrades and testing facilities among other projects. One of the means of providing funding for renewables is through the fossil fuel levy fund, which is now worth close to £200 million. However, that money remains unspent in an Ofgem bank account despite regular calls from Scottish ministers for action by the UK since May 2007. With independence we could unlock those funds to boost our green energy industry and deliver more green jobs.

We would also have the ability to exploit our potential for carbon capture and storage (CCS). Scotland is well placed to take a lead in the development and commercialisation of CCS with the knowledge and expertise in our universities and industry and our existing oil and gas infrastructure in the North Sea. However, many of the policies needed to make CCS a success fall to the UK government. We have been disappointed by the UK government's approach to CCS as so far demonstrated by the planned CCS pre-combustion plant at Peterhead. It was abandoned in 2007 and is now proceeding in Abu Dhabi. This is very much a lost opportunity for Scotland, due to delay and indecision by the government in London.

The oil and gas sector is central to meeting our renewables and CCS potential. Although it is a mature sector, Scotland's oil and gas industry is still of vital importance to our economy. There are a number of opportunities in the sector, such as promoting enhanced oil recovery, marketing the expertise of Scottish oil services globally, encouraging the diversification of skills, and the decommissioning and sustainable use of the infrastructure, such as for CCS.

Investing for the future

For many years the SNP has also called for better use of revenues flowing from our oil and gas wealth. The SNP wants to invest a share of the returns from oil and gas into an oil fund. This would allow a proportion of Scotland's revenues to be converted into an assets fund so that we can benefit from North Sea oil and gas long after it has gone. Many countries and regions have established oil funds or sovereign wealth funds, as Table 6 shows.

Table 6: Oil funds and sovereign wealth funds

Country	Fund name	Inception year	Assets ($ billion)
UAE – Abu Dhabi	Various investment funds	1976	656
Saudi Arabia	SAMA Foreign Holdings	n/a	431
Norway	Government Pension Fund - Global	1990	326
Russia	National Welfare Fund	2008	220
Kuwait	Kuwait Investment Authority	1953	203
UAE – Dubai	Investment Corporation of Dubai	2006	82
Libya	Libyan Investment Authority	2006	65
Qatar	Qatar Investment Authority	2003	62
Algeria	Revenue Regulation Fund	2000	47
Kazakhstan	Kazakhstan National Fund	2000	38
Brunei	Brunei Investment Agency	1983	30
USA	Alaska Permanent Fund	1976	27
Bahrain	Mumtalakat Holding Company	2003	14
Canada	Alberta's Heritage Fund	1976	12

Source: SWF Institute, Fund Rankings, April 2009

Norway first established its fund in 1996 and now has investments worth £274 billion. This is forecast to grow significantly in the years ahead (see graph overleaf).

Between 2009 and 2030 the remaining oil and gas reserves in Scottish and UK waters will be worth between £650 billion and £1.1 trillion. With Scotland's share of the revenue being estimated at 90 per cent the potential value of establishing an oil fund is still significant. An oil fund would deliver a substantial return from our oil and gas well into the future.

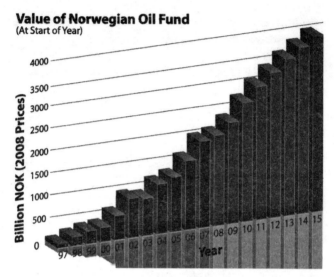

Value of Norwegian Oil Fund
(At Start of Year)

Source: *An Oil Fund for Scotland: Taking Forward our National Conversation*
(Scottish Government, 2008)

It has been said that Scotland has won the natural lottery twice, first with oil and gas and now with our vast renewables resource. That presents huge opportunities for our nation today and in the future.

Transport

As Scotland's government the SNP is working to create a wealthier and greener future. Improving Scotland's transport infrastructure is a big part of that ambition. We want to create a safe, integrated and efficient transport network that enables our country to be economically more competitive, improves connectivity and encourages Scots to choose greener transport options.

Our vision for transport in Scotland covers three major areas. We want faster rail journey times between our major cities. We want to make commuting easier, with more frequent train journeys, greater capacity and improved quality. And we are determined to ease road congestion by removing some of the well-known bottlenecks and completing our motorway network.

To deliver this vision we are investing £4.1 billion in Scotland's strategic transport networks over a three-year period – the largest investment in Scottish history. This is directly supporting much-needed jobs in our engineering and construction sectors and improving Scotland's economy through the more efficient movement of goods and people.

At the moment, the Scottish Government's transport agency, Transport Scotland, supports over a quarter of all the civil engineering sector's workload in Scotland. That is great news for businesses in this sector during the downturn and as we emerge from the recession. Nearly all of the agency's budget is invested to support private companies. In this way, we are creating hundreds of construction jobs across Scotland and sustaining thousands more across various industries. Indeed, our investment in infrastructure supports nearly 10,000 jobs across the road and rail sectors, with another 1,500 in maintenance projects.

Rail projects such as the Airdrie–Bathgate rail link and the Borders link are creating employment opportunities now and will boost local economies for the future. And recently delivered projects are making a tremendous difference to local communities across Scotland. The Stirling–Alloa–Kincardine railway is carrying three times the number of passengers forecast in its first year, and Laurencekirk station, which opened in May 2009, had 70 per cent more passengers than anticipated in the first four months of operation. These improvements for rail passengers are good for the local economies and good for our environment. We have no doubt that more rail passengers means fewer car journeys.

Road schemes such as the completion of the M74, the Aberdeen by-pass, the upgrade of the M80 between Stepps and Haggs and the completion of the M8 will make a big difference for travellers. It has taken fifty years for the M74 to be completed and so we are proud to have given the go-ahead for a scheme that will reduce congestion on the M8. That means fewer cars sitting in traffic jams pumping out pollution.

Some key parts of our strategic transport plan

- A new rail station at Gogar designed to integrate with the Edinburgh tram network and provide onward connection for passengers using Edinburgh airport.
- Electrification of the central Scotland rail network.
- Reducing Edinburgh–Glasgow journey times to 35 minutes, with twice as many services per hour.
- Delivering key components of the Aberdeen Crossrail scheme.
- The development of a metro/light rapid transit network across Glasgow.
- Faster, more frequent rail services linking Fife, Aberdeen, Inverness, Edinburgh, Perth and Glasgow.
- Reducing journey times between Inverness and the Central Belt by up to 30 minutes.
- Reducing Aberdeen–Edinburgh journey times by up to 20 minutes.
- Upgrades to the A96, including new Nairn bypass and new Inveramsay Bridge.
- Upgrading the A9 to dual carriageway standard between Perth and Inverness.

- Proposals for a new Dundee city bypass or upgrade of the Kingsway.
- Plans for a new national integrated ticketing scheme allowing people to travel across all public transport using just one ticket.

Looking to the future

We have set out our strategic priorities for Scotland's transport network with a programme of twenty-nine important national projects earmarked for the next twenty years, some of which are highlighted in the list above. These include the crucial Forth Replacement Crossing and the Edinburgh–Glasgow rail improvements programme.

The case for a new Forth crossing is clear and compelling. It is vital for maintaining an essential road link and supporting the economy of Fife, Edinburgh and the Lothians. The Forth Crossing Bill has now been laid before Parliament and parliamentary scrutiny of the Bill marks the next key stage as the project progresses.

The procurement process to build and operate the Borders rail link has now started. Re-establishing the line from Edinburgh to Tweedbank will provide communities in Midlothian and the central Scottish Borders with a direct rail route through to Scotland's capital – creating up to 400 jobs during the construction phase of the project.

And we are also investing more in rolling stock, with the biggest order in Scotland for a decade. This order, part of a total investment of over £430 million in rail services, will bring thirty-eight brand new trains, together with platform extensions which, along with improvements in the Paisley corridor, will help create over 130 new jobs.

The SNP is committed to continued investment in our vital national transport infrastructure. As budgets get tighter, we have to prioritise the projects that will deliver the biggest national benefit. In these challenging economic times this infrastructure investment not only creates jobs now, it also plays an important role in supporting Scotland's economy for the future. Of course we would like to do more. And we could, if the Scottish Government had the ability to borrow to finance capital investment. The SNP will continue to make the case for this, in government and through SNP MPs elected to Westminster.

And we will press Scotland's case for high-speed rail. At the moment the London government's plans suggest that Scotland will be left out of the first stage of the UK high-speed rail network, even though some of the biggest climate change benefits will come from delivering a fast link from the Central Belt to London. High-speed rail will also provide a significant boost to Scotland's economy, bringing us closer to markets across Europe. This is an important issue for Scotland, and with a strong SNP voice at Westminster we can make sure Scotland is not forgotten or left behind.

Rural Scotland

Scotland is a rural and maritime nation. Rural areas account for 95 per cent of our land and support 18 per cent of our population. Scotland's coastline makes up 10 per cent of the EU's total and we have a fifth of its seas. Our rural and maritime areas are critical to the economic, environmental and social fabric of our nation and make a significant contribution to the wellbeing of us all.

Scotland is famed throughout the world for its beautiful scenery and bountiful seas. Many of our sixteen million annual visitors come to experience our nation's natural beauty. Taking forward policies to help our rural and maritime communities thrive is therefore of central importance. Those who work on our land and seas act as stewards for the entire nation. They deserve our support to ensure economically successful and environmentally sustainable rural communities.

The importance we place on rural and coastal communities is reflected in the support we have shown over the years in the European Parliament, Holyrood and Westminster and by actions we have taken since becoming the Scottish Government in May 2007. Never before has Scotland had a government that places such importance on the success of rural areas.

The SNP in government

Since May 2007 the SNP has been working hard for rural Scotland across government. We have given our fishermen and farmers a stronger voice in Europe, with Scotland's case made more forcefully within the UK delegation and more directly to the EU itself.

And we are addressing many of the social problems facing rural communities. We recognise the distinct housing pressures in many parts of rural Scotland and so are enabling rural councils to build their first council houses in a generation. We have also introduced innovative schemes such as the road equivalent tariff to ensure vibrant and successful island communities. And we are protecting and restoring health services, extending rural broadband provision and providing a record number of police officers for towns and villages across Scotland.

Representation in Europe

The EU has an impact on the day-to-day lives of us all. Nowhere is this more the case than in rural Scotland. Europe has a central role to play in deciding policy on fishing, agriculture and rural development among other areas. A strong voice in Europe is vital to our rural communities. SNP ministers regularly attend council meetings to make the case for our rural communities. The SNP strongly believes that Scotland has distinctive needs that should be reflected at the top table in Brussels, especially in regard to rural and maritime issues. However, the UK speaks for Scotland, along with the rest of the United Kingdom. That means that Scottish ministers can attend meetings but are prevented from speaking.

Fisheries

The need for a strong voice in Europe is highlighted by fisheries policy. Since its establishment the Common Fisheries Policy has been a disaster for the economic and environmental wellbeing of our coastal communities and fisheries resources. Over the years centralised decision-making between member states – now numbering twenty seven and many of which are landlocked – has resulted in micromanaging the minutiae of fisheries policy. This approach has simply not worked. It has led to the shameful practice of discards – dumping perfectly good fish, dead, back into the sea, to ensure that skippers do not break crazy European rules. That is a scandalous waste of good food and our natural resources.

When the UK joined the EU, the London government described fishing as 'expendable' but for Scotland it is invaluable. Fishing contributes hundreds of millions of pounds to our economy every year and provides tens of thousands of jobs. Some £400 million worth of fish are landed in Scotland annually and we have about two-thirds of the entire UK industry. We need to ensure that we get the balance right between conservation of the resource, such as the Scottish Government's Europe-leading ban on the barbaric practice of shark-finning, and ensuring jobs, through encouraging diversity in the industry.

In spite of the restrictions there has been scope for improvements and Scotland's reputation as a leader in fisheries management continues to grow. At the end of 2008 the EU threatened significant cuts to Scotland's fisheries, including the closure of the entire west coast fleet. Instead of just accepting these cuts the Scottish Government, working in partnership with environmental NGOs and fishermen, introduced the conservation credits scheme. This has broken the mould, with its adaptive measures that encourage fishermen to undertake more sustainable practices.

The EU is currently looking at the future of fisheries in its Green Paper on the Common Fisheries Policy. This is a great opportunity for new thinking to ensure a future for our fishing industry and the coastal communities which depend so heavily on that industry. The Scottish Government is making its views clear and wants the EU to take the opportunity to return responsibility for fisheries to those who know how to manage the resource best. That would allow states to co-operate in managing this shared resource in a more sustainable manner, but without centralised control. That needs to happen as soon as possible so that we can put the disgrace of discards behind us.

Although our fishermen still face significant challenges we are proud to be able to work so closely with them on innovative proposals that can and will deliver more sustainable stocks. This is the sort of partnership, leadership and fresh thinking that Europe so badly needs. Co-operation at a European level is desirable in many fields, such as the fight against climate change, developing green technologies and the single market. However, the micromanagement of a very diverse fishing industry at that level is clearly nonsensical.

The marine environment

Scotland's marine environment is a vital resource. We hold a fifth of the EU's seas, containing well over 40,000 different marine species. The sea provides jobs and opportunities in a range of industries including fishing, aquaculture, renewables and oil and gas. That means careful managing. The Scottish Government has introduced the Marine Bill to ensure that we seek a balance in the competing demands of the sea.

With a quarter of the EU's tidal power and 10 per cent of its wave power our seas provide a massive opportunity for the marine environment. That needs to be balanced with the needs of other industries such as aquaculture. Scotland leads the EU in marine renewables and aquaculture, both innovative industries with a big future. The Marine Bill will ensure the careful and sustainable management of these resources.

Food and drink

Scotland's food and drink industry is growing fast and will become increasingly significant as food security attains ever greater importance. Since May 2007 exports and sales of Scottish produce within the United Kingdom have increased significantly. The industry is worth £10 billion to the economy and we have plans to grow that to £12.5 billion by 2017.

Much of the food and drink that we enjoy is produced close to our homes. We want to encourage more people to eat locally produced food. That is good for the local economy, good for health and good for the environment. That is why we have invested more in farmers' markets so that locally produced food is accessible to everyone.

In a speech in July 2009 to launch Scotland's National Food and Drink Policy, Richard Lochhead MSP, Cabinet Secretary for Rural Affairs, said:

> Scotland is a land of food and drink. That is why I am here today, at The Royal Highland Show, a showcase for Scotland's produce, to set out our recipe for success – the next steps of our national food and drink policy.
>
> Since we came to power just over two years ago, we have worked

tirelessly to promote the industry. And that's why we have worked hard in partnership with our primary producers, processors and retailers – right across the supply chain – to promote Scottish produce.

And our combined efforts are paying off. Consumers in Scotland and beyond are increasingly turning to Scottish produce because they associate the Saltire with quality, taste and loyalty to our producers. I can reveal today that independent research commissioned by the Scottish Government confirms the growing demand for Scottish food and drink.

And the results are striking. Retail sales of Scottish brands within Great Britain have increased by 21 per cent – that's over a fifth – since May 2007. That is a growth of £269 million. Sales of Scotch beef alone in Scotland have increased by 22 per cent, and sales of Scotch lamb in Great Britain have increased by 25 per cent. These figures are truly impressive. Our retailers, producers and processors are to be congratulated.

And one retailer told me that, so far this year, their sales of Scottish produce have already exceeded the whole of last year. Another told me they recently replaced one supplier of tomatoes from elsewhere in the UK with a Scottish supplier and, thanks to the Saltire on the label, sales immediately shot up by 25 per cent. The Saltire effect is delivering a premium worth millions to the Scottish economy. This success confirms our view that food and drink has a big future and will deliver many benefits for our people.

The prize here is a great one – a healthier, wealthier and more environmentally sustainable Scotland. Let's seize the opportunity.

Agriculture

Scotland's farmers, crofters and other land managers have a particularly important role given the rural nature of our nation. They maintain our landscape as well as ensuring the security of our food supply. In Scotland there are particular challenges as much of the land has Less Favoured Areas status.

Rural communities depend on the success of agriculture to provide jobs. It is the economic backbone of many of them. It is important that these communities get the support that they deserve. The SNP wants to see farmers continue to receive payments through the Common Agricultural Policy (CAP). This includes support through, for example, the Single Farm Payment scheme. In government we have set up the Pack inquiry to explore and address how we ensure farmers and taxpayers get the best value for money from these schemes. In contrast the UK government wants to see this sort of support phased out. Its report on the UK's vision for the future of the CAP confirms that this approach would lead to a decrease in livestock numbers and farmers' income.

We are determined to ensure that those managing the land in our most remote areas get the right support. That is why we increased payments to those farming Less Favoured Areas, a substantial section of our agriculture industry. Crofting is an important part of farming in these areas. Our aim is to tackle absenteeism and neglect so we can ensure the future success of some of our most fragile communities. We have listened to the views of the crofting communities in taking forward our crofting legislation. It is based on the recommendations of the Shucksmith inquiry and will help us build a successful crofting industry fit for the twenty-first century.

What more we can achieve

The Scottish Government is already delivering for rural Scotland. However, we cannot achieve all we would like to without adding to the current responsibilities of the Scottish Parliament.

Rural Scotland is heavily influenced by decisions made in Brussels on topics such as aquaculture, fisheries, marine conservation, agriculture, forestry, animal health and welfare, biodiversity, waste, recycling, water management, protected food names, pollution and climate change. The Scottish Government provides a stronger voice than ever before but could do so much more with a direct voice. Our view is that Scotland should have the same rights and access in Europe as nations like Ireland, Finland or Denmark.

Today, the Scottish Government is responsible for implementing EU decisions, but we are limited in the ways we can influence them. Full membership of the EU would bring a seat at the top table, the Council of Ministers. We would have a commissioner and double the representation in the European Parliament. That would allow us a stronger voice when the key decisions are being made. We would be better placed to make the case for rural Scotland and its unique needs.

Scotland's lack of a direct voice has certainly held us back in the past. It has damaged Scottish interests. Over the years it has led to a succession of damaging decisions such as the Common Fisheries Policy. With two-thirds of the UK industry, fisheries is a priority for the Scottish Government in a way that it just is not for the UK overall.

At present Scotland receives about €360 million under Rural Development funding, which compares to €2.1 billion for Finland and €2.3 billion for Ireland. Scotland is the lowest in the European league table in terms of funding for utilised agricultural area.

As a full EU member, we could secure a better deal and avoid decisions that fail to take into account Scotland's unique situation. A good example is the electronic identification of sheep, signed up to by the previous Labour–Liberal Democrat administration in 2003. The Scottish Government has made progress negotiating some flexibility and we have allocated £3 million to help the industry. As a Member state government, rather than a devolved government, we would have been in a stronger position to say no to this European proposal.

Having our own representation and voice in Europe would also allow us to speak up in other areas. For instance, the Scottish Government has significant concerns about the spread of genetically modified (GM) crops, along with many other EU member states, but we are represented by the UK, which consistently votes in favour of GM.

Extending the responsibilities of our parliament would allow us to develop the policies best suited to Scotland's rural communities. For instance in marine policy the devolution settlement means that issues such as coastguard, lighthouses or health & safety are reserved to the UK along with many of the responsibilities relating to the renewables and oil and gas industries. These could and should become the responsibility of the Scottish Parliament so we can deliver a more integrated marine policy framework.

It would also allow us to develop a fairer deal for our farmers. For example the Scottish Government cannot currently create a supermarket ombudsman to ensure that there is a fair deal for all of those involved in the food and drink supply chain. This is a decision that rests with Westminster at the moment and Westminster has not been willing to act. We think it would be so much simpler if Scotland could just take this sort of decision itself.

The SNP recognises that rural Scotland is one of the engine rooms for the success of our entire nation. It supplies the basics of life to us all through its industries from food on our tables, the water in our taps and the energy powering our homes. It deserves the policies that will ensure its success in the years to come and it deserves the strongest advocates at Westminster, in Europe and here in Scotland.

Defence

Defence policy in the United Kingdom is reaching a crucial point. Our forces have been involved in two wars for well over five years, and this, together with the continuing operation in Afghanistan and Labour's mounting deficit, have all put tremendous pressure on our forces, their families and the Ministry of Defence's budget. This will present significant challenges and raises many important questions about the direction of defence policy in the United Kingdom.

What is certain is that, whoever wins the UK general election, there will be a Strategic Defence Review which will look at all aspects of defence policy, from strategy to the structure of the armed forces, funding and equipment. One problem is that past reviews have failed to properly anticipate new trends and circumstances, and the result is that UK defence policies and capabilities have always lagged behind in a changing world.

An important part of any review is to incorporate the key and undisputed facts about current defence spending, military capability and footprint, including here in Scotland, and to reverse a trend that has seen Scotland losing out from UK defence policy

What we need now is a Scottish defence review, because it is abundantly clear that UK policy is leading Scotland in the wrong defence direction, with virtually no public support. This policy involves a dramatic decline in the conventional defence footprint, at the same time as planning to impose a new generation of Trident nuclear weapons in Scotland, albeit in possibly diminished form. Pressures on military service personnel and their families at the present time are unprecedented. Dangerous tours of duty in

Afghanistan, general military overstretch and a changing society have contributed to major challenges. All of these realities and pressures are reflected in the public's desire for a review. A special YouGov poll commissioned by the SNP revealed that almost three-quarters of Scots support a Scottish defence review.

It is vital that a Scottish review ensures that defence policy reflects Scotland's priorities and preferences and is focused on the future.

UK defence and Scotland

It is only recently that the Ministry of Defence has started to make estimates of how much it spends in each nation of the United Kingdom. There has been a lot of rhetoric from other parties about the supposed benefit Scotland gets from UK defence spending, but the actual picture revealed by the MoD is shocking.

Thousands of defence jobs have been cut in Scotland since Labour came to power in 1997 and there has been a multi-billion-pound defence underspend north of the border, as well as a litany of base closures and regimental restructuring. The abolition and amalgamation of the historic Scottish regiments and the dissolution of the 'Golden Thread' are the most visible manifestations of UK defence cuts in Scotland. Recent defence job losses and closures in Scotland include:

- RAF Lossiemouth – 1,040 service jobs terminated, 50 civilian jobs phased out
- RAF Leuchars – 160 service jobs terminated
- RAF Kinloss – 180 service jobs terminated
- HMS *Gannet* – 245 service jobs and 107 civilian jobs lost
- RAF Stornoway closed – 23 service jobs terminated, 5 civilian jobs terminated
- Moorings and Support Depot, Fairlie closed – 50 service jobs lost
- Royal Naval Storage Depot, Rosyth closed – 200 workers laid off

- RAF Machrihanish passed to Defence Estates – 128 service jobs terminated
- Army Depot, Forthside, Stirling closed – 12 jobs terminated
- RAF Buchan closed – 55 civilian jobs lost and 200 RAF jobs relocated.

These cuts represent a loss to local communities and together have had a significant impact on the Scottish economy. Compared to 1997 there are now 6,480 fewer civilian and service jobs. In addition another 4,000 jobs based on direct MoD expenditure went between 2003 and 2007. This brings the total number of lost jobs to at least 10,480 since 1997. In terms of service personnel England is the only nation to have enjoyed an increase since 1997, of 1,000. The YouGov survey found people in Scotland were quite clear, with a majority of more than two to one in opposition to defence personnel and bases in Scotland being run down.

In addition to job losses, it is now clear that there is a significant defence underspend in Scotland. Answers to parliamentary questions received in the last year reveal that Scotland receives far less than its 8.4 per cent population share. Between 2002 and 2007 the actual underspend revealed was £4.3 billion.

What these statistics show is that Scottish taxpayers are contributing significant sums towards the UK Ministry of Defence, but they are not seeing the economic benefit of that investment.

The way ahead

People in Scotland support our armed forces and are proud of the nation's military tradition. We are angry, however, at decisions taken by the UK government to put our troops into the illegal conflict in Iraq, to underequip them in Afghanistan and to waste billions on new nuclear weapons.

Having full responsibility for defence matters would let the people of Scotland decide these issues. We would have been free to decline to take part in the recent Iraq War, based on its lack of a legal mandate. And we would be in a position to ensure the removal of nuclear weapons from Scotland.

We have a moral objection to nuclear weapons and we also believe that when the UK government is planning cuts in Scotland's budget, it should not be wasting £100 billion on buying a new generation of nuclear bombs. The nuclear deterrent has an employment costs as well. Research conducted by the Scottish TUC and CND found that the money spent maintaining the UK's nuclear deterrent costs Scotland approximately 3,000 jobs.

Faslane, the current nuclear submarine base, should be the base for conventional naval forces. This is the approach adopted by similar, independent nations. Norway, for example, supports a conventional naval fleet and conventional bases with more people employed as civilians or service personnel than the current position in Scotland. Independence would allow us to make similar choices.

At present there are only three Air Force bases in Scotland and one naval base. Less than half of our locally recruited army units are based in the country. We will retain current facilities to accommodate conventional forces in Scotland, while co-operating with our neighbours in procurement, training and basing.

Our near neighbours in Scandinavia provide clear examples of what independent countries can do in defence policy. Co-operative projects have already taken place, including advanced planning for a Swedish and Norwegian unified overseas force, and the Swedish Defence Minister, Steg Tolgfors, is discussing common military forces in northern Sweden and Norway including shared air bases. He said: 'There are an incredible number of areas in which the two countries could work together, even though Norway is outside the EU and Sweden is not a member of NATO.' This could be a model for partnership and co-operation on these isles.

Scotland would become a member of NATO's Partnership for Peace (PfP) programme. Such co-operation would bring the benefits of close working relations with NATO members and would allow Scotland to participate in missions, exercises and synergies like heavy airlift, when it was in Scotland's best interest, while remaining outside NATO's command structure and the nuclear elements of the Alliance.

Non-NATO countries co-operate with NATO in the International Security Assistance Force mission in Afghanistan. In this United Nations-mandated mission, non-NATO countries that are in the PfP, for example Sweden, take part in the NATO-led mission alongside countries such as Australia, which is not in the PfP or NATO. These are the sorts of choice that would be available to an independent Scotland.

Today Scotland has limited involvement in defence decisions, but where we do have responsibility, for example over veterans' affairs, we are acting to great effect. We have extended NHS priority treatment so that all veterans with a condition associated with military service receive the same access as war pensioners. We have also established the Scottish Veterans Fund, which will help a variety of projects across the country, and are delivering free bus travel to all injured personnel by 2011.

A vote for the SNP in the upcoming general election is a vote against MoD job cuts. It is a vote for a strong voice in London to demand that Scotland gets its fair share of defence expenditure. It is a vote for a proper Scottish defence review to develop a proper plan for Scotland's defence priorities. It is also a vote to send a bloc of Scottish MPs who will be powerful advocates for Scotland's priorities and Scotland's values – saying no to the obscene presence of nuclear weapons on Scotland's shore and no to billions being spent on new weapons of mass destruction.

Finally, a vote for the SNP is about choice. The SNP want

Scotland to have the same opportunity as other, similar nations so we can become a country that develops a defence policy that is right for Scotland and that makes Scotland a force for good in our changing world.

Foreign affairs

One of the defining characteristics of the last century has been the flourishing of independent nations all around the world. Since 1900, 143 countries have declared independence and taken their rightful place in the international community. These declarations haven't been limited to the years immediately after the Second World War – indeed the last two decades have seen twenty-eight countries join this community. Increasingly, independence is the natural state for nations like Scotland.

These countries have responsibility for their relations with other countries and their overseas activities are designed to bring maximum benefit for the people and businesses of their own nation. They can decide, like Ireland, to focus international efforts on trade promotion, engagement with the diaspora and on overseas aid, or, like the UK, can focus instead on status and the projection of power.

Scotland currently has no say over the approach adopted on our behalf by the UK. For example we must be part of the UK line on nuclear weapons at non-proliferation talks even though the UK position of spending as much as £100 billion on new nuclear weapons goes against the opinion of the majority of Scots.

And in Europe we have only limited influence on UK votes and the UK negotiating position even though these may damage Scottish interests and Scottish jobs. For example, the United Kingdom and Scottish governments have fundamentally different views on reform of the Common Agriculture Policy (CAP). The UK wants the entire 'First Pillar' of the CAP, which delivers income support for thousands of Scottish farmers and farm businesses, to be phased out. We believe this approach will undermine large parts of Scottish agriculture given that about 85 per cent of Scotland falls under the European Union's category of Less Favoured agricultural land, where profitability is lower. With our own overseas representation and a seat at the top table in Europe, Scotland could work to protect the interests of important Scottish industries.

'Stop the world, Scotland wants to get on' – Winnie Ewing, November 1967

Scotland can be proud of its role in the international community. People from across the globe have strong connections to Scotland. Scottish culture, manufacturing and produce are all well known throughout the world. Scottish troops have served in operations around the globe with distinction. Scottish aid and aid workers have offered a vital lifeline to some of the poorest people in need.

Sadly at present Scotland is held back because almost all foreign policy matters are reserved to the UK. The contrast with other nations is stark.

In Europe, similar-sized countries such as Denmark and Ireland have more representatives in the European Parliament and they enjoy the many benefits of being a full member state including representation on the key Council of Ministers, where the most important decisions are taken. These nations would not choose to have their interests represented by one of their neighbours. They are part of the debate, part of the decision-making process, when

Scotland, in contrast, is forced to sit on the sidelines. The SNP believes that Scotland should be an equal member of the European Union and should, like Ireland, Sweden, Finland, Denmark and the rest, enjoy the many advantages of full representation.

And we believe Scotland should be involved, as of right, in other important international debates. Scotland, which has the most ambitious climate change legislation in the world, was excluded from the Copenhagen summit in December 2009. The UK government made a clear and deliberate decision to deny Scotland a voice even when we had a world-leading story to tell. That is not good enough.

A principled approach

The SNP's approach to international relations would be based on principles that define Scotland as a nation: compassion, fairness and humanity – and as such the SNP will always uphold the rule of international law.

We support the right of democratic nations to pursue, together, common efforts to defeat terrorism and believe that any global military response should have proper UN sanction. This, we believe, will help ensure that in fighting the extremists we also uphold the human rights that are an essential part of our freedoms. Indeed it is these human rights that we are fighting to protect. At the 2009 SNP conference, Alex Salmond said:

> As a party and as a government, we will stick firm to our principles. And without fear or favour, we will take the big decisions. Even in the face of the most terrible atrocity, the most severe provocation, we can put mercy before retribution.
>
> We all recognise the suffering of the families of the victims of the Lockerbie bombing. What they have experienced no family, no person, should ever endure. But the evil of terrorism thrives in the darkness of fear and shrinks from the light of compassion. It is right that Mr

al-Megrahi was tried and convicted for his crimes, but it is also right that he has been sent home to die.

Last week Arun Gandhi came to see me – the grandson of Mahatma Gandhi. He seeks with our Scottish churches to found a reconciliation centre in one of our great universities. One of the things that he told me is that his grandfather's philosophy is much misunderstood. His resistance was not passive but active. His dedication to non-violence is a strength, not a weakness. Sometimes someone has to break the cycle of retribution with an act of compassion.

Peace and prosperity

An independent Scotland will contribute towards international peacekeeping, international development and humanitarian missions. And with an SNP government, an independent Scotland would meet its obligations to international development projects. This stands in contrast to the high rhetoric of successive UK Labour and Tory governments. They failed to reach the international standard of 0.7 per cent of national income for overseas development, in contrast to nations such as Denmark, Sweden, the Netherlands and Norway.

An independent Scotland would make international development a priority. As the Scottish Government since 2007, the SNP has doubled Scotland's international aid budget and is building strong links with Malawi and other sub-Saharan nations. With responsibility for our own international development budgets, we would be able to channel more cash into projects, making a real difference in the Third World, where the focus of the Scottish Government has been on education and health.

The SNP believes that Scotland should join with the world community where necessary to preserve peace and security. We propose a Scottish Centre for Reconciliation and Conflict Resolution, to promote peaceful alternatives to armed conflict.

With the full responsibilities of independence we will be able to guarantee that Scottish soldiers are never again dragged into an illegal war waged against the wishes of the Scottish people. The Scottish Parliament will always have the final say on whether our servicemen and women take part in any military conflict.

Playing our part in the global climate change challenge

The SNP wants Scotland to play a leading role in the global battle against climate change and we are doing all we can to work with other countries to ensure the long-term security of our environment.

The Scottish Parliament's climate change legislation is the most ambitious in the developed world and we are engaged with partners across the globe because this Scottish standard should become the world's standard. We have set the bar high with our actions and our legislation and believe the world can and should follow. Our world-leading position in key green energy technologies forms a central part of our overseas representation activities. In Europe we have already secured a place for Scotland in the development of the crucial North Sea Supergrid – a project that will allow clean, green energy from off Scotland's shore to flow to markets in Europe, and internationally, through the Saltire Prize, we are positioning Scotland as the place to be for the development of this potentially planet-saving technology.

These are exciting times for Scotland. We have a major contribution to make. Much can be done today, and so much more can be achieved with the full responsibilities and flexibilities of independence. A vote for the SNP will mean Scotland's voice is heard loud and clear on these issues of global importance: on war and peace, international aid, climate change and economic opportunity. We will ensure Scotland's values and priorities cannot be ignored.

Afghanistan

The SNP has major concerns about the UK government's approach to the current conflict in Afghanistan. With the death toll rising we question why our soldiers are there without the equipment they need and without a clear strategy for delivering peace or democracy. Once again the men and women on the frontline are doing us proud, while the leaders back in London are letting our soldiers down.

In 2001, the SNP supported international efforts, backed by the UN, to defeat al-Qaeda and their Taliban hosts. However, after the initial success, we believe that the US and UK took their eye off the ball in Afghanistan, as a result of the invasion of Iraq. The conflict in Iraq weakened international action and the international coalition in Afghanistan. Resources and expertise were directed to Iraq and as a result the situation in Afghanistan got progressively worse.

The invasion of Afghanistan was a fair and proportionate response to the terrorist atrocity of September 11. The SNP welcomed and emphasised the importance of a broad international approach and the need also to deal with the fundamental factors that had allowed terrorism to thrive.

Two key points were important to us from the very beginning. We argued strongly that Afghanistan was not a conflict that could be won by narrow military means alone and that military intervention should be conducted in a manner that did not conflict with broader humanitarian aims in the region. And we made clear that the central involvement of international organisations, such as the UN, was vital in giving international legitimacy to the operation in Afghanistan.

Supporting our troops on the ground

The SNP is working hard to ensure that the UK government meets its obligations to our soldiers serving in Afghanistan.

A key part of this effort has been ensuring that troops have adequate equipment and the safest and most effective transportation in what is difficult and dangerous terrain. We have consistently sought to bring to the public's attention the failure of the MoD's procurement regime to provide troops with the necessary equipment. We have scrutinised notable failures which have included the initial inability to equip Merlin helicopters with the necessary protective Kevlar armour and the delay in getting armoured vehicles into theatre.

As the SNP's Westminster leader, I have shared the concerns of service personnel about shortages of the transport helicopters necessary to keep troops off the ground, where they are susceptible to roadside bombs. Given the failures outlined above, in a conflict that has now lasted longer than the Second World War, it is wrong that there has never been a full strategic review of military operations in Afghanistan. We believe that an approach that fuses the civic and humanitarian goals in Afghanistan with a rational military strategy is necessary. Such an approach has, so far, been lacking. The inability of the British government and the MoD to provide the coherent strategy we need as the conflict has unfolded has led to the tragic loss of service personnel and, unsurprisingly, to a sense of public disenchantment.

What next in Afghanistan

The SNP wholeheartedly agrees with the view taken by Jeremy Greenstock, the UK's former ambassador to the UN, that while the army has been 'holding up a wall', this is unstable without the buttress of development. Indeed any military advances that may be made are undermined by the fact that Afghan civilians are seeing

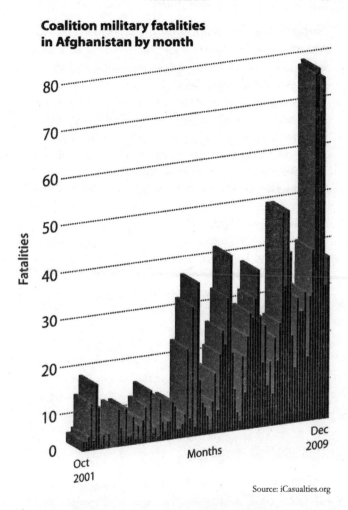

Coalition military fatalities in Afghanistan by month

Source: iCasualties.org

little in the way of reconstruction and redevelopment on the ground. A broad-based developmental approach must also incorporate a political solution that includes engaging in dialogue as appropriate in order to offer an alternative to violent conflict.

Across the world, combating poverty and the underlying causes of conflict is an essential part of the broader strategy we need. Such an approach will reduce the need to intervene militarily in the future in countries such as Afghanistan.

The SNP has welcomed President Obama's detailed statement and vision for future engagement in Afghanistan, given in November 2009. We believe the UK government now also needs to raise its game and we are urging ministers to undertake the sort of exhaustive strategy review carried out by the Obama administration.

Ultimately the SNP does not wish to see Scottish troops committed indefinitely, without being given a sense of their overarching goals. Without a clear vision of what is being fought for, and a without a consideration of the means that will be necessary to achieve such an end, the UK's commitment to Afghanistan is likely to remain deeply problematic and continue to lose support from the public in Scotland, the UK and, importantly, Afghanistan itself.

Health

In 2008 the NHS in Scotland celebrated its sixtieth anniversary, and it has focused our attention once again on the support that the founding principles of the NHS continue to enjoy across Scotland.

The SNP's approach is clear. The NHS in Scotland should always be a service that is publicly owned and delivered. Its unified structure embraces patients and the public as co-owners of the service rather than consumers in a competitive marketplace. The absence in Scotland of an internal market puts a focus instead on collaboration and co-operation. We also reflect the strong opposition in Scotland to privatisation in the NHS. Apart from at the margins, there is no significant private sector delivery of NHS care in Scotland – and this reflects the approach we believe delivers most benefit for patients.

Our decision to fund the new £842 million Southern General Hospital in Glasgow entirely from public capital also illustrates our opposition to the 'one for the price of two' delivered previously through PFI – an arrangement that squeezed the money that was available year in, year out to support patient care.

Working for a healthier Scotland

The SNP government has been working hard to deliver improvements in the NHS and we recognise that what has been achieved could not have been done without the effort and dedication of the staff throughout the health service.

- We have cut waiting times, so that patients are now receiving outpatient, inpatient or day case treatment within eighteen weeks.
- We have abolished hidden waiting lists – so that thousands of people who were previously exempted from the benefits of waiting times will now be seen and treated within the eighteen-week target.
- We have worked with local partners on reducing delayed discharge, meeting the target to eliminate all delays over six weeks.
- We have reduced the rates of hospital-acquired infections and increased spending on tackling infections by 260 per cent.
- We have protected under-threat A&E services at Ayr and Monklands Hospitals.

And we know that a healthier Scotland is also about reducing health inequalities, which is why we are phasing out prescription charges – a tax on ill health – for all by 2011, with the biggest reductions already for those with chronic conditions who need regular medication.

In April 2009, in a speech on tackling hospital acquired infections, Nicola Sturgeon, Cabinet Secretary for Health and Wellbeing, said:

Nothing is more important to me personally than driving down the rates of infection in our hospitals. Hospital infections cause pain, distress and suffering for patients and their families. And they undermine confidence in our NHS. That is why beating them is a battle I am determined to win.

And we are making progress. MRSA rates are down since we came to office. And I can report to you today that, in the last year, rates of *C. difficile* have fallen by nearly 20 per cent. That is progress but it is not good enough. We must do even more. Hospital cleanliness is of the utmost importance. Patients have a right to expect the highest standards and let me be clear that, on their behalf, I will not accept anything less. That is why I have set up a new inspectorate, headed by a chief inspector, to police standards in our hospitals.

And it is why I told you at our last conference that I was banning any further privatisation of hospital cleaning contracts. But I intend to go even further. I can announce today that we will make the resources available to employ an extra 600 hospital cleaners across the NHS in Scotland.

And the people of Scotland can rest assured that these will be cleaners working in the NHS, for the NHS, and employed by the NHS. There will be no Labour privatisation of cleaning services by this SNP government.

This investment is good for the NHS and good for patients. It will improve even further the standards of hygiene and cleanliness in our hospitals. But it will do more than that. At a time of rising unemployment, it will also provide jobs for 600 people. More practical action from a government on Scotland's side.

Looking to the future

We have developed a new strategy for health in Scotland, Better Health, Better Care, which sets out in detail the SNP's vision in government for a more mutual NHS. A mutual NHS is one in which patients, the public and staff are seen as co-owners of the health service, with the rights and responsibilities that go with that status. The policies that will bring it to life are many and varied – pilot elections to NHS boards; a new Patients Rights Act and strengthened partnership working at local and national level. Our approach has at its heart a strong commitment to participation and involvement: to the participation of patients as partners in their own care, and to the involvement of patients, the public and staff in the design and delivery of health services in the future.

People in Scotland have a passion for and pride in the NHS. That is why we are focused on delivering a new era for patient and public participation in Scotland's NHS. It represents a step change in the power, influence and voice that the Scottish public will have in our NHS. It recognises the public not just as consumers with rights but as owners of the NHS, with rights and responsibilities. It represents a radical shift towards an NHS that is truly publicly owned.

This concept of mutuality does not mean a change in the financial or structural arrangements of NHS Scotland. But it does mean gathering the people of Scotland, our voluntary and community sectors, all of our partner organisations and the staff of the NHS around the common purpose of building a healthier Scotland, a common purpose that will be delivered through integrated care and co-operation. It involves a genuinely collaborative approach to healthcare that builds on the founding values of the NHS and rejects the market-based model favoured elsewhere in the UK.

In building this mutual NHS, we are taking forward a Patients' Rights Bill, which will include waiting time guarantees and the right of patients to be treated as partners in their own care. We are putting in place independent scrutiny of major service change, building on our experiences of the independent scrutiny panels already established in the Ayrshire & Arran, Lanarkshire and Greater Glasgow & Clyde health board areas to ensure the most appropriate decisions for local health provision. And we will produce and distribute an annual 'ownership report' to every household in Scotland. This will set out the rights and responsibilities of patients and their carers alongside information on how to access local services and raise issues or complaints

Better health for all

Our approach is also about reducing health inequalities in Scotland. Our nation's health is improving, but it is improving faster in the wealthiest sections of our society than it is in the poorest. As a result, health inequalities are widening. We believe that, in a country as rich as ours, that is simply not acceptable.

Health improvement requires a long-term commitment. The full value of the work we do to support children may not become apparent until that child has become a parent or a grandparent. But there is action that the NHS can take now to create the conditions in which people have the confidence, motivation and ability to make healthy choices.

We believe that every extra pound spent encouraging people to stop smoking, tackling alcohol-related harm or supporting drug rehabilitation is a pound wisely spent. That's why we are investing more in these services, including an additional £85 million over the next three years to combat alcohol-related harm with a greater focus on changing behaviour.

We can and must make the biggest difference in the long term – by giving our children the best possible start in life. Work emerging from across the world shows that the circumstances in which a child is brought into the world can have a major impact on physical and mental health. It is therefore critical that we give our children the best possible start by supporting good health choices and behaviours that will help them to remain well throughout their lives. The key to this approach has been the development of a cross-government early years strategy. That will provide the framework within which we and our partners will deliver effective support for children and young people and it is why we are extending entitlement to free, healthy school meals and increasing nursing and other healthcare support in schools.

Over the past sixty years, the NHS has secured its place at the heart of Scottish society. We have set out a hugely ambitious agenda to keep it there, striving for a mutual NHS that promotes health, tackles inequality and leads the world in patient safety.

Safer communities

Most of Scotland's communities are great places to live, work and bring up a family. Yet some of them, too many of them, are still blighted by anti-social behaviour and some are plagued by serious crime. When the SNP came into office in 2007 we had a difficult legacy to deal with – Scotland's streets were not as safe as they should have been.

Our approach is to focus on two key elements. First, to get tough on the causes of crime, which means that we must deal not only with manifestations of crime but with the factors that so often contribute to it: drink, drugs and deprivation. We must instil a culture of responsibility: individuals must take personal responsibility for their actions and face the consequences. And government and communities must also play their part so that together we can face down the criminals and thugs. Second, we know that the best route to fighting crime is to have more police officers in our communities and more specialist crimefighters able to tackle specific issues such as street violence, drugs and serious and organised crime.

Tackling crime

Tackling the fear of crime and deterring criminals requires effective front-line policing. A visible police presence deters crime and reassures communities. We are therefore looking to deliver additional policing capacity – more police officers spending more time in our communities and on the beat. By cutting unnecessary bureaucracy, working smarter and using new technology our police forces are better equipped to meet the complex challenges of modern policing.

And to support this smarter working the SNP in government is delivering more police – an additional 1,000 police officers in the lifetime of this parliament. Currently, the number of police officers in Scotland is 17,217 – 983 more than when we came to office. The underlying trend is clearly very strongly upwards. Between June and September 2009, 271 new officers were trained at the Scottish Police College.

South of the border it was reported in 2009 that large numbers

Police Officer Strength in Scotland
2007-2009

Bar chart data:
- Q1 2007: 16,234
- 16,265
- 16,306
- 16,267
- 16,221
- 16,339
- 16,526
- 16,675
- 17,048
- Q2 2009: 17,278

Quarters Q1 2007 to Q2 2009

Source: *Police Officer Quarterly Strength Statistics Scotland*, 30 June 2009

of police forces are planning to cut thousands of officers. In contrast the SNP is delivering record numbers in Scotland.

And just as we have a record number of police, we also have the lowest crime levels in a generation. In 2007/8 the police recorded a fall of 8 per cent in recorded crime and an increase in the clear up rate to 48 per cent. Overall conviction rates remained high, at 89 per cent of those proceeded against, and the average length of a prison sentence has increased by 7 per cent according to the latest figures.

Violent crime

Too many communities across Scotland are scarred by the booze
and blade culture. In some parts of the country this makes it difficult
for us to enjoy our public spaces and a night out on the town can
be a less than pleasant experience, especially at closing time. For
too many people, knives are seen almost as fashion accessories, not
the killers that we know them to be. That's why we are taking new
initiatives to direct police efforts against those who carry knives.
We are supporting the excellent work of the national Violence
Reduction Unit, including record levels of investment. One of the
most high-profile initiatives of the unit has been to use airport-style
scanners at railway stations and clubs to target those who could be
carrying knives.

Effective policing is only part of the solution. In Glasgow a
team of senior medics, who see the full impact of knife attacks
week after week, are visiting schools to deliver a hard-hitting
message about the risks and dangers of carrying a knife. And we
are supporting the Community Initiative to Reduce Violence, which
is an intensive project focused on 600 identified gang members to
change their behaviour

And those who are caught face a tougher response from the
criminal justice system. More knife carriers are being sent to jail and
they are getting longer sentences. The average sentence for those
sent to prison for carrying a knife increased from less than four
months in 2003/4 to well over seven months in 2007/8.

Organised crime

Organised crime causes misery. It undermines legitimate businesses
and damages our national economy. The gang bosses profit at the
expense of us all.

In January 2008, in a speech about tackling the 'godfathers' of
crime, Kenny MacAskill, Cabinet Secretary for Justice, said:

For too long the gangsters of the criminal underworld have been able to direct their evil enterprises and operate with apparent impunity, profiting on the backs of decent hard-working Scots and their families.

This government has already made clear its determination to tackle serious organised crime in all its forms. That includes the criminal kingpins, as well as their lieutenants and the footsoldiers who do their dirty work. We are working together with the police and other law enforcement agencies to put these criminal networks out of business.

In 2007 we established a Serious Organised Crime Taskforce to ensure that all the key law enforcement agencies are working to fight organised crime. Our strategy was launched in June 2009. It sets out four objectives, which will guide our actions: to Divert, Detect, Disrupt and Deter the criminal gangs. And we are making sure the gangs do not profit from their crimes. Assets are being seized and the money handed back to the communities that have suffered. Cashback for Communities will invest over £13 million in a range of projects for young people. We are working with national partners to deliver sporting and artistic opportunities for thousands of young Scots.

We are giving £2.5 million to the Scottish Football Association, £4 million to YouthLink, £1.4 million to Scottish Rugby Union, £600,000 to Arts and Business Scotland, £1.7 million to Scottish Sports Futures in partnership with Basketball Scotland, £2 million to the Sports Facilities Fund and £1.2 million to the Scottish Arts Council and Scottish Screen. All this allows more than 100,000 young people to benefit from money seized from criminal gangs. More is being seized every year and we will make sure communities continue to be paid back for the crimes committed.

Dealing with drugs

Drugs are at the root of much of Scotland's organised crime and many of Scotland's social problems. They are the great social challenge of our age. That's why we are working to cut drug supply and demand. We are bringing together partners across the public sector – in the police, NHS and councils – with a focus on recovery for addicts. Our aim is to help those Scots who, whether because of low self-esteem or lack of opportunity, shoot up and opt out. We have the first Scottish drugs strategy in ten years and are backing it up with record investment. This funding will go directly to NHS health boards for drug treatment services across Scotland and will help to fund recovery services which will be tailored to local needs. We said we would increase investment in frontline drug services by 20 per cent and we are delivering.

Prisons

We believe prisons should be for serious and dangerous offenders and not for fine defaulters or the flotsam and jetsam of our communities. That means we need to shift the balance and end the revolving door that sees low-level offenders moving in and out of prison. We want them to face tough community punishments that will not only deter them from crime, but also help them find a route out of crime. These tough community punishments – community payback orders – will protect the public, help offenders to turn their lives around and include some clear payback to the communities that they have harmed.

There will be a presumption against prison sentences of six months or less. That does not mean a blanket ban – judges will still be able to impose such sentences if they feel that no other option would be appropriate. If someone has committed a serious crime or is a danger to the community they should not be getting a prison sentence of less than six months.

The reason for this new approach is simply that the old way

wasn't working. Three out of four people sentenced to six months or less in prison will offend again within two years. That is not making our communities safer. In contrast, 42 per cent of those sentenced to community service have a clean record after that time.

David McKenna, chief executive of Victim Support Scotland, has said: 'I think this is a golden opportunity really to take a radical and new view of how we deal with crime in our communities, making it better for communities but more importantly making it better for victims.' We think he is right. The other parties support a system that sees thousands of criminals released only to offend again. We think they are wrong.

Ending Scotland's unhealthy relationship with alcohol

In March this year Scotland celebrated the fourth anniversary of the ban on smoking in public spaces. This is a perfect example of what can be achieved when our nation and our political parties are prepared to come together and show collective leadership. It's time to adopt the same approach to the misuse of alcohol.

The scale of the problem

There is no doubt that alcohol misuse is costing Scotland dear. A report by Audit Scotland in March 2009 estimated the financial cost at £2.25 billion a year or £500 for every adult in the country. In

January 2010 a report from academics at the University of York suggested the figure could be substantially higher, at £3.56 billion for the nation as a whole or £900 for every Scottish adult.

However, the human cost in terms of damage to health is even more alarming. Enough alcohol was sold in Scotland in each of the last three years to enable every man and woman over sixteen to exceed the sensible male weekly guideline on alcohol consumption each and every week of the year. Drinking above the Chief Medical Officer's recommended guidelines increases the risk of lasting health damage and there is clear evidence that increased consumption is driving increased harm. There were more than 40,000 hospital discharges in 2007/8 due to alcohol-related illness and injury, and alcohol-related mortality has more than doubled in the last fifteen years.

Scotland has one of the fastest-growing rates of liver disease and cirrhosis in the world (see graph opposite). The Chief Medical Officer has now added alcoholic liver disease to the list of 'big killers' in Scotland, alongside heart disease, stroke and cancer. Alcohol-related illnesses could be killing as many as one in twenty Scots – twice as many as previously thought. It means that one Scot is dying from alcohol-related causes every three hours. We need to act urgently if we are to reverse the harm to our health, our families and our communities that misuse of alcohol is causing.

Action on alcohol misuse

It's time for effective action. There is no one single solution to this problem, there is no silver bullet. Rather, it will take action on a number of fronts to rebalance Scotland's relationship with alcohol, including action to raise the price of the cheap, high-strength products that are at the root of so many of the problems we now face. That's why we propose a minimum price for each unit of alcohol. It is simply unacceptable that one can exceed the male weekly guidelines for less than £3 and the guidelines for women for just over £2.

Chronic liver disease and cirrhosis rates in men, 1950-2006

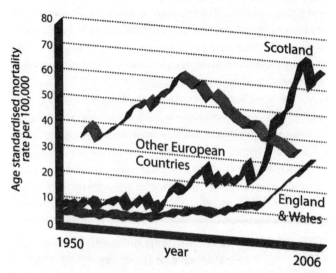

Source: *Changing Scotland's Relationship with Alcohol: A Discussion Paper on Our Strategic Approach* (Scottish Government, 2008)

There is much international evidence that shows the price of alcohol and consumption is linked: if the price is low, consumption increases; if the price is high, consumption decreases. There is also strong evidence that shows increases in harm are driven by increased consumption. A World Health Organization report from 2009 titled *Evidence for the Effectiveness and Cost-effectiveness of Interventions to Reduce Alcohol-related Harm* stated: 'There is indisputable evidence that the price of alcohol matters. If the price of alcohol goes up, alcohol-related harm goes down.'

Making Scotland safer and healthier

In October 2009, a study published by researchers at the University of Sheffield showed that minimum pricing would save hundreds of Scots' lives every year, cut crime and improve Scotland's quality of life. Our proposal is expected to have economic benefits as well – including nearly 30,000 fewer absence days from work every year and significant yearly savings for taxpayers. The key points from the Sheffield University study are as follows:

- Harmful drinkers would pay an extra £137 per year, compared to just £11 for moderate drinkers.
- Harmful drinkers' consumption would fall nearly 9 per cent (294 units of alcohol), equivalent to 118 cans of strong lager/cider or eleven bottles of vodka per drinker per year.
- Total alcohol consumption across society would fall 5.4 per cent, concentrated among hazardous and harmful drinkers.
- Alcohol-related deaths would fall by about seventy in the first year and 365 annually by Year 10 of the policy – a reduction of nearly 19 per cent.

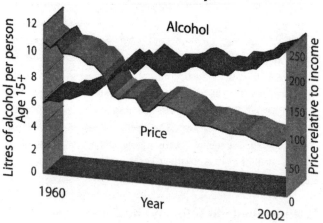

Relationship between price and alcohol consumption 1960-2002

Source: *Changing Scotland's Relationship with Alcohol: A Discussion Paper on Our Strategic Approach* (Scottish Government, 2008)

- Alcohol-related illnesses would fall by 1,200 in the first year and 3,700 annually by Year 10 – a reduction of around 8 per cent.
- General hospital admissions would fall by 1,600 in the first year and 6,300 annually by Year 10 – a reduction of nearly 10 per cent.
- A fall in crime of 3,200 offences per year.
- Nearly 30,000 fewer workdays lost through absenteeism and 1,250 fewer people unemployed because of alcohol misuse per year.
- A financial saving from harm reduction (health, employment, crime etc.) of £60 million in Year 1 and £950 million over ten years.

Following the publication of the study, Nicola Sturgeon, the Cabinet Secretary for Health, said:

> These findings confirm that minimum pricing can be a key weapon in the battle against alcohol misuse. That's why the Scottish Government has included it in a package of measures which, taken together, could have a significant impact in reducing Scotland's alcohol misuse burden.
>
> Minimum pricing will not raise the price of all drinks – it will target products sold at rock-bottom prices which are harming our health and our communities. Those who are damaging themselves and others by bingeing on dirt-cheap alcohol will be hit hardest, while moderate drinkers will be almost completely untouched.
>
> While minimum pricing is not the whole answer, sensible drinking starts with sensible pricing. We have to listen to the evidence if we want to start cutting the cost of alcohol misuse to families, communities and our economy.

Stephen House, the chief constable of Strathclyde Police, has made clear the impact of low-cost alcohol on crime levels. He said: 'We've got to have price control on drink. We've got to drive up the price so that it's not as cheap as it currently is in supermarkets. That will control people's behaviour and we support that.' And a study by the former governor of Barlinnie prison, Bill McKinlay, in October 2008 found that 56.8 per cent of offenders said their actions had been fuelled by drink, compared with 40 per cent in 1996 and 29.5 per cent in 1979. The study also found that, at the same time alcohol consumption increased, the proportion of young offenders involved in serious violence, including murder and attempted murder, rose from 22 per cent in 1979 to 53 per cent in 2007.

The SNP understands the scale of the challenge in pursuing a policy of minimum pricing. Breaking new ground is never easy, as we saw with the smoking ban, but evidence and support is building to the point where the chief medical officer of Scotland has claimed that 'when you look at the facts, introducing minimum pricing is a no-brainer'. In fact, all the UK chief medical officers support it, and they were backed in January 2010 by the House of Commons Health Committee. The committee's report on alcohol said: 'The evidence showed that a rise in the price of alcohol was the most effective way of reducing consumption just as its increasing affordability since the 1960s had been the major cause of the rise in consumption. We note that minimum pricing is supported by many prominent health experts, economists and the Association of Chief Police Officers. We recommend that the government introduce minimum pricing.'

The Welsh Assembly considers that 'the evidence for the introduction of a minimum price for a unit of alcohol is now overwhelming'. And it looks like some in the UK government are now also moving towards minimum pricing. We know that such a measure would save thousands of lives and improve the wellbeing of the country. But, as we have always said, there is no single solution – indeed we believe minimum pricing will only be fully effective if taken forward as part of a comprehensive package of measures.

We have backed our policies with record investment of £120 million over three years. In our framework we make clear that we are routing the bulk of this investment in services through NHS boards so that they can deliver services that best meet local need. Indeed we have put our money where our mouth is on tackling alcohol misuse – more than £60 million across Scotland invested directly in services over two years, compared to £10 million per year under the previous administration.

We are working together across government towards the long-term goal of changing culture and behaviours around alcohol. Recently the new Licensing Act came fully into force. This updates the current system, which dates back to the 1970s, and provides the most comprehensive and ambitious package of licensing reform Scotland has ever seen.

We are aware that Scotland's drinking culture will not be changed overnight. We face a major challenge in addressing alcohol misuse in Scotland, but the time has come for action. We have been clear that as a party, we are in this for the long term. The eyes of the world are on Scotland and we must make the right choice.

A new age of responsibility

Throughout this book, responsibility has been a central theme. As a party we believe that Scotland will only reach its full potential when we take responsibility for our own future with independence. And this belief in national responsibility is seen also in our wider approach.

As individuals, as communities and as a nation, we must take responsibility for our own success – responsibility for building the wealthier, fairer, greener, safer and healthier country we know our nation can be. And it is a responsibility that goes hand in hand with true social justice and real opportunity for all.

The past decade was an age of irresponsibility, whether in the economy, national finances, foreign affairs or the global climate, and now we are all paying the price.

The decision to take our country to war in Iraq on the basis of false information has cost lives and left our nation and the world less safe. The UK's obsession with nuclear weapons means that we will spend £100 billion on new weaponry when money is being cut from crucial frontline services. In Scotland, because of the legacy of the Private Finance Initiative, repayments will soon reach £1 billion a year, reducing the resources available to invest in jobs and education, in health and wellbeing. The folly of PFI has meant we get one hospital or school for the price of two – it has been like buying a house on a credit card rather than with a mortgage.

Today, the UK finds itself facing a huge and growing debt burden. Not enough was done in the good years to bring the deficit under control. Between 1980 and 2008 Britain borrowed £672.5

Angus Robertson MP, SNP Westminster leader, House of Commons, July 2009

It is essential that we move to a trustworthy system – and the Scottish Parliament sets the benchmark on how that can be done. It is essential that Westminster matches Scottish Parliament standards of transparency, including the introduction of criminal penalties against MPs who break the rules on expenses or fail to properly declare financial interests.

The Scottish Parliament has shown the way with legal sanctions that can be applied against wayward parliamentarians, and Westminster must introduce the same sanctions against MPs that break the rules

We now need to get on with the independent audit of the last four years of claims so that MPs' accounts can be cleared or otherwise, and we get on with the urgent process of restoring public confidence.

billion, with the Scottish share of this debt amounting to £56.5 billion. And yet over this period Scotland was in financial surplus 50 per cent more often than the UK – a much stronger position – and indeed Scotland has had more years of surplus since 1980 than the UK has had since 1963.

If we had been able to keep all the tax raised in Scotland and still maintained the same level of spending, our debt over this period would have been just £23.5 billion – over £30 billion less than our share of UK debt today. We have allowed irresponsible UK financial management to burden each and every Scot with more than £6,000 of unnecessary debt.

It is time for a new approach and that means a new age of responsibility here in Scotland. We can choose a future that sees us save our huge energy wealth with the benefit felt not only today, but by generations to come. We can decide not to waste billions on grandiose projects like ID cards or new nuclear weapons and instead invest in those areas that will make the biggest difference to everyday life – decent pensions, local services, improved infrastructure or health, education and skills. These are choices we cannot yet take, given the limits that are placed on Scotland and the Scottish Parliament with devolution, but we could take them with independence. The Scottish Parliament has allowed us to achieve much already, but there is more we could do. And that is why we must extend and complete the parliament's powers.

The Scottish Parliament has grown over these past ten years. From a difficult start, with public anger over expenses and the cost of the Holyrood building, it is now delivering legislation that has changed and will change our nation for the better. It represents a new politics – a more open, accountable and consensual approach that provides all parties with a role to play.

We believe that Scotland would be better served if all decisions about our future were taken by the Scottish Parliament but in the meantime we also know that Holyrood offers important lessons for Westminster as it now faces public anger over expenses and growing calls for fair votes. In these areas, the Scottish Parliament provides a 'gold standard', with stricter rules and greater openness on expenses, and a voting system that means the parliament has the real power and can more effectively hold government to account.

Much has been achieved but there is more to do. Whether in the City and the financial markets or in the House of Commons, the old ways must come to an end. They have not served our nation well.

At this election we cannot afford more of the same. Scotland's voice must be heard. Scotland's interests and Scotland's values – Scotland's many and diverse communities – must be at the fore.

That is true of the debate in the weeks ahead and crucially of the decisions that will be taken in the new parliament.

That means it is more important than ever to have strong local and effective representation, working for Scotland and standing up for the issues that make a difference to everyday life.

Together, Scotland's got what it takes to become one of the big success stories of the twenty-first century. We have no doubt about our nation's talents and opportunities. With your help we can build a better nation and create this new age of responsibility and success. Your vote will make a difference.

A vote for the SNP is a vote for strong local champions and a vote to put our communities and Scotland first.

About the author

Angus Robertson MP is the Westminster Leader of the Scottish National Party.

He speaks on Defence and Foreign Affairs for the SNP and has twice been nominated as the Best Scottish Politician at Westminster.

His Moray constituency, between Inverness and Aberdeen, contains the whisky-producing heartlands of Speyside and is home to two military airbases.

Angus Robertson managed the SNP's victorious 2007 Scottish Parliament election campaign, which secured the first ever Nationalist administration at Holyrood and installed Alex Salmond as First Minister.

Prior to his election, Angus worked as a foreign and diplomatic correspondent in central Europe for the BBC, Austrian Radio and other leading broadcasters.

Angus, who is half German, was born in London, brought up in Edinburgh and studied at Aberdeen University. He is married, lives in Moray and is a keen hobby cook.